Untethered
A Memoir

Untethered

ISBN: 979-8-9876745-1-2

Book design by Mary Elizabeth Gillilan
Painting by William F. Wakeling
Author Photograph by David W. Wakeling
All other photographs are from
Elizabeth Jane Pryce's private collection.

Published by the Blue Bottles Writing Studio
Bellingham, Washington

Dedication

This memoir is dedicated to women everywhere who stay silent. Raise your voices and sing, even if it is out of tune. To my birth mother, for enduring the trauma of shame and having to give up her firstborn. Thanks to my maternal grandmother, "Mummy," for raising me—her humour, idioms, and proverbs gave me a solid foundation for life. I would not be who I am without both my mothers. Most importantly, I want to thank my three children, who often experienced neglect due to my frustration and anger at not being heard, yet still care about me. Each has grown into an accomplished adult.

I am proud of you.

Acknowledgments

I want to thank all my wonderful early first readers and editors. I deeply appreciate their enthusiasm, countless hours of reading, and positive advice: Rita Saling, Kate Birr, Ingrid Rees, Elga La Pine, and my daughter, Sarah Willett.

I also want to thank my fellow writers in the Blue Bottles Writing Studio and those in the Monday group at Mary Elizabeth Gillilan's Independent Writers Studio. Thank you for listening to me read and motivating me to write better.

Finally, an extra thank you to Mary Elizabeth Gillilan for her graphics and patience with putting the book together.

About the Author

Elizabeth Jane Pryce has lived in Bellingham, Washington, since 1991. She was born in the seaside town of Bridport, Dorset, England, in 1949 to a single mother but was raised by her grandparents in the Caribbean Islands until the age of fourteen. Elizabeth Jane left her island home for England, believing she would return within a year.

Instead, Elizabeth Jane found herself in a family as the eldest of her birth mother's children. To survive emotionally, she lived a double life, an internal one of sadness, missing her grandparents, "Mummy and Daddy," and an external life crammed with as much activity as possible.

Elizabeth Jane's stories in the following pages chronicle her life in England. Her undaunted spirit shines through the painful reckoning of a marriage breakup while raising three children, renovating houses, and earning her college degrees.

She is the author of *Wild Child* (2010), a collection of poems about the influences of her early life. Her poetry has appeared in *Clover, A Literary Rag,* and a poem in *Borders: An Anthology of Stories*, and *Corridor,* a free monthly zine of poetry and art. She is one of four independent authors who published *The Blue Bottles Writing Studio: A Variety of Stories* (2020) as part of a writers group she still organizes and runs. Elizabeth Jane Pryce is the author of *Chosen, A Memoir* (2022) about her childhood growing up in the Caribbean.

2022
Choices We Make
An Overview

"What have you done to your hair?" These are the first words my ninety-three-year-old mother says when the WhatsApp video springs into action. It is her first afternoon home after breaking her hip less than a month ago.

We have only said a few words to each other in the last month, as calling a patient in an English hospital is nearly impossible. Wi-Fi rarely works inside the walls of the building. My youngest sister, Sophie, made an effort and added a small amount of data to her phone service. She called during our mother's second week in the hospital. I only managed to say, "Glad to hear you are doing so well," and a few moments later, "I'll talk to you again soon," before the phone sputtered and died.

So here we are, more than two weeks later, and before I can say anything, I am triggered by the sharpness of her voice. I am certain she is criticising my appearance. "I cut it," I reply curtly, thinking, *you have no control over me.*

She is the only mother I have now, and sometimes, I struggle to maintain contact, wanting her to feel cared for but not wanting to feel angry at her. "Mummy," the parent who raised me until I was fourteen, passed away over thirty years ago, and "Daddy" over forty years. In many ways, I consider myself an orphan, but I do not tell anyone that.

About ten years ago, I decided I didn't want to let my birth mother, Althea (or Thea, as I call her), die without trying to forge some real connection between us. My reasons are selfish. I am her eldest daughter, and I don't want to feel any remorse when it's her time to leave this earth. One of Mummy's sayings was, "Never let the sun go down on your anger." I am no longer angry at Thea, but I am still curious why she treated me so unfairly. Was I difficult? And, if I was a reminder of her trauma, why did she have me live with her?

I grew up in the Caribbean with Mummy and Daddy from the age of nine months. I didn't know they were my grandparents until I was taken back to England at fourteen. I ended up living with my birth mother and her other children instead of returning to St. Vincent in the Caribbean—the story I was told before I left my island in the sun.

Looking back over those years in England, I am aware of an anger in me that grew steadily stronger. It started with apprehension in the early 1960s when I first went to live with my "new" family. It escalated to a determined resentment by the end of the 1960s after being expelled from Thea's home several times and accused of unkind and false misdeeds. My rage became explosive by the late 1980s, twelve years into my marriage and a young family. I had never heard of counselling back then—I felt my identity disappearing.

In the spring of 1985, a year before Mummy died, I secretly signed up to take an Access Course, which, if I passed, would allow me to take a four-year bachelor of arts course at a college in London. It was a decision that changed our lives forever.

The results of that decision were overwhelming, empowering, thrilling, and motivating, but also traumatic. My family thought I was crazy. Even Mummy said, "How will you manage? You have a husband and three children to take care of. You have a duty to them first."

I was brokenhearted but quietly unwavering in my need to get the degree. I had met and had a brief, incredible relationship with a young man living in our house. As wrong as an affair is in a marriage, it felt like a gift from God. I came alive to the possibilities I held, still dormant, within me. It was as if I had been born anew. I listened to music, went to the theatre, wrote poetry again, and read serious books. College was once again in my sights. Strangers and friends around me noticed and commented on my metamorphosis, all except my husband, in-laws, and my birth mother. Only Mummy said, "You look happy. I'm glad."

In September 1985, after completing the Access Course, I was excited to be accepted into the Polytechnic of London, now known as the University of London for a BA in English.

The following October, on my birthday, Mummy passed away. Before Christmas that year, my husband and I had a significant altercation over our dog, which resulted in divorce. He moved onto a barge on the Thames near Richmond. It was a choice he'd wanted me to make a few years previous, to which I replied, "No, not with three children." And, "Where would I put a sewing machine?"

In the summer of 1986, I made the trip of a lifetime. I took the children, ages nine, seven, and five, to America. We traveled through thirteen states, seeing many of the Wonders of the World: Niagara Falls, the Tetons, Yellowstone, and the Grand Canyon, to name a few. We were invited to join families for picnics in the park and learnt the word "potluck." We were occasionally invited to spend the night as guests in strangers' homes. I even went tubing on a lake in Eastern Washington. Wherever we went, people talked to us and asked us about ourselves. This was something that rarely happened in England. There, a person is an island unto himself. The outside world does not intrude. As we headed home from Seattle, my daughter summed up our feelings, "If it wasn't for Maureen (her hamster), I wouldn't want to go home."

None of the children mentioned their father or grandmother during our travels. We took on American idioms, like bathroom instead of W.C. or loo. I even drove on the right-hand side of the road without any problems.

Bellingham, our last port of call, felt like home. What I heard and saw reminded me of the freedom I had known growing up as a child in the Caribbean. I wanted to live in this town. It would take another five years, but I made my choice—I was determined to move six thousand miles away from my family and start a new life again with my three children in Bellingham. "Mummy" often used to say, "As you make your bed, so you must lie in it."

The Christmas before we left Parkholme Road, I invited my whole family to celebrate. I hoped to reconcile the joy and the tears of our past struggles. Old pictures show a happy gathering. I talked with my siblings, played with nieces and nephews, and went to bed happy, feeling my "gifts of love" had worked their magic. Everyone seemed happy. I had hoped for acceptance, gifts of books, maybe, and encouragement to continue going to school. What I got instead was a beautiful cut glass cake plate from Thea. It felt like a slap in the face. It said, "Know your place—don't try to be what you are not." A few days later, I received another slap. Thea called and reproached me for my selfishness. I could not fathom what I had done except be happy.

England:

They Do Things
Differently
There

1964
Aboard the *Parthenon*

In January 1964, my sister Lorna, who I soon discovered was my aunt, flew to St. Vincent in the Caribbean. Together, we sailed back to England on the Van Geest shipping line for what I believed would be a year.

The ship, *Parthenon*, was a freighter carrying bananas from the Caribbean to the United Kingdom. Lorna and I were two of six passengers on board. The other four were two retired colonial couples. One husband and wife were returning to "good old Blighty" (England) after a lengthy period in Hong Kong. As a final "hurrah" before retiring, the British colonel and his wife had spent a month touring the Caribbean. She was quiet, smiled at me often, and said I was "a good girl."

At the dinner table, the colonel talked in what I later discovered were spoonerisms, a linguistic flip-flop of words that turns a slip of the tongue into "tips of the slung." He completely confused me, and Lorna's responses didn't help much. I thought spoonerism was a strange word because the colonel never used any spoons. He was amusing, but it was hard to follow anything he said.

The other couple was returning from imperialist India. This husband also had a funny way of talking. He used abbreviations instead of words. I never understood what he said. But he gave me some sulphur cream for an abrasion, which healed a weeping sore on the soft area below my shoulder blade within days. His wife taught Lorna and me how to play canasta.

Our first days were calm and beautiful. The sun shone, and the passengers lounged on the deck. The adults read books, wrote letters, or played deck games. When the sea was rough, everyone stayed inside. Although I liked watching the sea spray fly up over the stern and cover the deck, I didn't appreciate our plates sliding across the table. I didn't enjoy rolling out of bed, either. One night, Lorna packed me tightly into the bunk with blankets and pillows on either side of me. Another night, our cabin chair danced across the room. It reminded me of travelling from Montserrat to St. Vincent aboard the *Maracas Bay*. Mummy, Daddy, and I wedged across the cabin with our trunks and Wong, our cat, who never made a sound. It made me sad. I missed Mummy and Daddy, as well as my dog and cat.

On my first day at sea, I met Ben, a good-looking young German sailor. Every time I saw him, he winked, causing me to giggle. After dinner one night, feeling sad and lonely, I returned to the cabin early. Lorna stayed in the dining room, talking with the other passengers. After cleaning my teeth, I tried to get into my bunk, planning to read for a while, but I couldn't get my feet in between the sheets. After struggling and failing, I finally got up and pulled the bedding off completely. I gasped and laughed out loud as a fat, shiny apple and a couple of oranges rolled out onto the floor. My sheets had been folded back on themselves as a practical joke, which is why I couldn't get into bed—a "tight apple-pie bed" or short sheeting.

Ben must have been standing outside the door because he knocked right after I stripped the bed.

"*Sie* put *Apfel* in *dein* bed?"

"I think you did!"

"*Hast du* problem?"

"You tied my bed in knots," I giggled.

"Me? *Nich*. Not me," he laughed.

"I know it was you," I said.

I thought Ben was funny, and I laughed, listening to his accent while watching his pantomime of me trying to get into the bed. I hadn't laughed so much since playing "Hands, Knees and Bumps a Daisy" in the kitchen with Mummy and Daddy. It made me want to cry again.

"I'd better get into bed now or my sister may find us and be cross with me," I said. "You'd better go."

"*Gute Nacht*, Jane," he said, bowing low at the waist, and almost falling on his nose.

I laughed so hard that I almost choked.

"*Komm mit* me in the morning? I take you to see *das* ship, *ja*?"

"Oh! Yes, please, I would like that very much."

Ben was a few years older than I. This voyage was his first time away from home, too. He told me later he had an older brother and a little sister. He said I reminded him of her. He was the youngest crewman, and I was the youngest passenger, so we were naturally drawn to each other.

I could hardly contain my excitement when Ben arrived the next day after lunch to show me around the ship. The engine room was amazing. It was big, with large pipes and wheels, and very noisy. It was unlike any of the small boats I had sailed on before. I met the cook and a couple of other men in the galley. They wore white pants, jackets, and chef hats. The galley was small, with shiny pots and pans hanging from the ceiling. Ben's cabin was so tiny we couldn't stand in the room together. It was the smallest room I had ever seen, besides the doghouse* on the *Lady Angela* when Mummy and I first went to Trinidad.

In the eight days following the apple pie bed incident, we met in the stateroom for a few hours after Ben finished his duties on board. We played different board games from the special box I had received for my 12th birthday. I liked checkers best, especially as I won most of the time.

After suppers, I excused myself from the dining table, saying, "I'm going to our cabin to read." Ben was more fun than the other passengers at the table, with their peculiar ways of talking. He always left me little gifts under my pillow, sometimes a single wrapped chocolate or an apple. He occasionally tied knots in my sheets when he made the bed earlier in the day. I never told Lorna. I knew she wouldn't understand. She definitely wouldn't laugh. She didn't seem to think anything I said or did was funny. I only saw her laughing at the dining table with the other guests.

On the night the dinner plates slid off the table, Ben brought me some crackers with an apple and cheese, which was tasty. I washed it down with

---

*A raised protective hut on the deck for sailors to sleep in.

18

pineapple juice while Ben sat on the chair by the bunk. He chatted in broken English about his day on the ship and how much he liked playing the games with me. When I finished eating, he left in case Lorna returned and found him there.

Ben and I played hide and seek around the ship when he wasn't working. One time, I hid in our cabin bathroom. When I felt the door rattle. I hung onto it, thinking it was Ben. It was Lorna, and she was annoyed with me. She spoke crossly, "Come out at once, you silly girl."

The last time Ben and I met, it was different. He made lemonade, poured it into two pretty stemmed wine glasses, and handed one to me. I remembered the special glasses Mummy and Daddy had kept in the mahogany and glass cabinet at home. They had matched the crystal bowl that always sat on the fragrant cedar press.

"Link your arm through mine and drink to us," Ben said softly, then a little louder, "*Brüderschaft*." ** He continued, "Kiss me, Jane."

I kissed him on the cheek.

"*Nein*, here," he said, touching his lips.

Our eyes locked as our lips touched in a soft kiss. I felt the room swirl away, and my spine tingled from top to bottom. I heard Ben whisper "*Brüderschaft*" again, and I forgot everything else.

** A German drinking ritual to consolidate friendship.

England and Winterdown

I woke on the morning of January 20th and realised we had finally arrived in England. We were actually at the Barry docks in Wales, a vital seaport facility in the Vale of Glamorgan, on the North shore of the Bristol Channel.

I dressed as quickly as possible. I wore shop-bought undies for the first time— Mummy had always made my panties with pockets. I was happy never to lift my skirt again to reach my hankies. I struggled to put on the thick dark blue wool skirt and pink cardigan Lorna had brought to St. Vincent for when I arrived in England. The clothes were heavy and itchy, but I loved the tiny pearl buttons on the cardigan. The black stockings and the suspender (garter) belt that held them up were difficult and uncomfortable. I refused to wear the plum coat with the black fur collar; it was too heavy. I felt it would drag me to the ground. I only weighed sixty-five pounds and stood under five feet tall. I also wanted Ben to recognise me when I left the ship.

I had barely fastened the last clip of the suspender belt when I felt the ship's soft banging against the dock tyres and heard the engine stop. We were about to step onto solid land after nine days at sea. We disembarked around 9:00 a.m. to the loud sounds of cranes moving heavy crates and packing boxes. They swung over the rails and landed heavily on the ground. Men ran everywhere, releasing ropes and shouting orders in unfamiliar yet pleasingly musical voices.

Unlike at home in St. Vincent, there were no little boats with Black men rowing us out to the large ship in rainbow-oiled waters. I didn't see a Black man or woman anywhere. It felt strange, foreign. It surprised me how much I missed their presence—their shiny Black bodies, rippling muscles, and sing-song voices.

Standing at the top of the gangway, I could see our trunks sitting on the dock. "Look, Lorna, our trunks!"

"Hush, Jane. It is not ladylike to shout."

Halfway down the gangway, I turned, delighted to see Ben standing at the ship's stern. He saw me, and we waved to each other before Lorna hustled me forward. "Come along, Jane. Behave yourself. It isn't ladylike to turn around like that. We have to hurry, there is no time to dawdle," she chastised. "We have a train to catch."

I was crestfallen by Lorna's reaction to my excitement and dismayed by the weather. Although it was wintertime in England, I saw no white fluffy stuff on the ground. Mummy had often talked about snow, and I was eager to see some. It would be April before I saw any.

Lorna hailed a taxi to take us to Cardiff Station, where we caught a Pullman train to Paddington, London. From there, we took the underground to Waterloo. I was disappointed because it didn't go underground. Francis, Lorna's husband, met us for the last part of our journey—Waterloo to Esher and a taxi to the house. It had been a long day. We didn't reach Winterdown, Lorna and Francis's home, until late evening.

After only one day, Lorna caught a train to London, "I have some business to take care of," she said.

I wandered around the house, lonely and miserable. I wished I could magically transport myself to the *Parthenon* with Ben, or better still, back to my island home.

By the second week, Francis took me in hand. He was a lot more fun than Lorna. We worked in the garden, cut down trees, and went for long walks. I told myself to stop being a crybaby. This year would be an incredible adventure.

Winterdown was an old house in the middle of a large area of the Metropolitan Green Belt in Esher, Surrey—forty miles outside of London.* The driveway to the house started at the A3 (now the A307), which runs from Esher to Cobham. The driveway was gravel, moss, and grass, which, if Francis hadn't cut regularly, would have turned back into a woodland. A red fox's trail ran alongside the driveway; Francis and I often watched the fox in the early morning mist.

The River Mole, a tributary of the Thames, ran along the bottom of one side of the property. The river rose in West Sussex, near Horsham, and flowed northwest through Surrey for fifty miles until it reached the Thames at East Molesey, opposite Hampton Court Palace. Sometimes, I saw, or at least heard, canoeists

---

*The Metropolitan Green Belt is a statutory green area around London. It is a largely undeveloped, wild, or agricultural land. The first green belt around London was ordered by Queen Elizabeth I in 1580. It was a three-mile-wide belt created to stop the spread of the plague.

as they paddled by. They were practicing for the great annual race from Devizes to Westminster.

I still believed what I was told—I would go to France with Lorna and Francis. While they captained their beautiful, fifty-foot motorboat, *Wairakei II*, on the canals of France for wealthy tourists, I would go to a boarding school. I was excited to learn French. Then, best of all, we'd sail back to my beloved home with Lorna, Francis, and David, a close friend—just the four of us on a sailing ship on the immense Atlantic Ocean.

I wasn't at Winterdown long before I noted in my diary that a young couple and their children came to visit. It was Saturday, February 1st. Lorna introduced them as "my baby sister, Thea, her husband, Don, and my niece and two nephews."

It appeared that while I was playing and enjoying the countryside at Winterdown, a conversation, or argument most likely, happened between Lorna and Thea. Although it concerned me, I was not included in the exchange. The family left, and Don returned alone the next day. Lorna said, "Go and collect your things, dear. Don is taking you to stay with Thea and the children in Crawley for a while. You'll continue coming to Winterdown every weekend."

I lived for those weekends. I had grown up on a small island with elderly parents and no siblings. I was eager to leave the noise and constant activity of family life in Crawley. On Saturday mornings, I would depart from the house after breakfast and walk to the railway station at Three Bridges, about half a mile away. I'd catch a train to Croydon, then another to Surbiton, and finally change again for Esher. The journey took at least two hours, but I enjoyed the freedom of travelling. At Esher, I would catch a bus to what is now called the Winterdown Road and walk up the driveway, arriving in time for lunch.

I spent the weekend roaming through the woods or going to the river, pretending I was back on my island. I loved the bluebell woods best. It was a large area below a high escarpment above the River Mole called Lover's Leap. The trees, the woods, the bluebells, and the river at Winterdown were my solace. There, I could dream, create stories, and pretend I was somewhere else. Occasionally, I visited the family at the bottom of the hill to play with their two young children.

I loved winter evening teas in the sitting room at Winterdown. Lorna liked to serve crumpets covered in melted butter. It was a tea-time special I never had before. Sometimes, it was a lovely slice of fruit cake instead of crumpets. As we ate, I would stare into the crackling fire and look for images with delight.

My New Home

When I moved into Thea's home with her family, I was the oldest of four children, with another to be born soon. Once the baby arrived, we were two adults and five children living in a three-bedroom house. I was the outsider and treated as such on the sly by the oldest boy, Derek, who was eleven. Tina was the sweetest little girl and loved having a big sister, but she loved taking the beautiful costume jewellery

Mummy had given me. The youngest, Jimmy, was quiet and seldom involved in childish arguments or fights—I hardly noticed him. We were too young to understand the emotional upheaval we were experiencing. Displacement in the hierarchy of children within a family is rarely a good thing. Once, when Thea asked me to hold the baby, Sophie, she tried to suckle from me. I was so horrified that I avoided spending time with Sophie until she could walk and talk.

It had only been a few months since leaving Mummy and Daddy in the Caribbean. There, I was an only child of doting older parents. I had a room of my own and friends. I enjoyed roaming the hills and rivers with my dog and playing teacher or doctor with my dolls. Now, I shared a room and had nothing familiar from my island in the sun. I felt my freedom disappearing.

I was only at school for a few days, before we came down with chicken pox, starting with Derek. Back home in St. Vincent, Mummy gave me lots of care and attention when I was sick. Now, I was one of four children, and attention was divided. I slept for the best part of a week. After I felt better, I looked at pictures, went to the Girl Guides with Thea, and played board games with the children. I cut out and sewed dresses for myself, made a lot of tea at the church for the elderly of the community, and visited Lorna and Francis on the weekends.

Diary entries from that time consisted of meeting Thea and Don's friends, walking to school with their children, enjoying the two youngest children coming into my bed in the morning before school, and playing football with Derek almost every day. Don seemed kind. Once, he insisted on buying me a pretty dress.

Although it was fun to be around the other children, I found it difficult to be in my new school, Hazelwick, especially as I was shy and came from a place no one in my class had ever heard of. After having chicken pox, I contracted mumps and did not return to school for eight or nine weeks, which put me at a further disadvantage. The school assessed me as having average intelligence, a low grasp of maths, and no ability in foreign languages compared to the other children my age. I overheard the headmaster say my mental age was around nine years, although I was over fourteen.

At St. Joseph's Convent in St. Vincent, I learnt Castilian Spanish, which Hazelwick didn't offer; they only taught French. A year later, when they did introduce Spanish, they said I would be too far behind to start a language. I was placed in the 3rd year "B" stream.

English comprehensive schools in the 1960s placed children in one of three groups, or "streams," each year according to their aptitudes and abilities. The "A" stream was considered top-grade and university material. The "B" stream would finish with a General Certificate of Secondary Education (GCSE) qualification at sixteen plus years of age and could go on to complete further academic achievements. The "C" stream students were deemed incapable of additional tuition and would leave school at sixteen without further accreditation. I felt lucky not to have been assigned to the "C" stream.

Three years later, with the headmaster's encouragement, I entered the Upper Fifth (US senior year). I would finish my schooling with a slightly higher qualification, a Certificate of Secondary Education (C.S.E), at the end of the school year. Thea and Don refused to let me continue into the Sixth Form to take my "A" levels exams. That would have qualified me for admission to a university education. They wanted me to work and contribute to the household.

Although we lived only a twenty-minute walk from Hazelwick, Don continued to insist on dropping me off at the school gates in his car on his way to work. Unfortunately, riding with him often made me late. After I was given a detention for being late to school several times, I finally persuaded Thea and Don to let me walk. The other three children were in the local primary school, opposite the small shopping parade—a row of small businesses. They always walked.

I took the shortcut along the path behind their school. Even though, according to Thea, I wasn't supposed to because I might be caught by a "weird man." I was scared, but I would stop at the top of the alley, clutch my satchel tightly under my arm, fill my lungs with air, and run, ready to scream if any man confronted me.

I had only been back in school a few days since recovering from chickenpox and mumps. I was already tired of children and teachers who eyed me as though I was a strange creature, saying, "You talk so funny?" Those children made me cry and feel lonelier. There were no other overseas children in the school. Everyone

I met was born in Crawley or moved there when young. It was a new town, built as an overflow from London. Many young couples moved there to provide a better place to raise their families.

First Snow

It was Easter and my usual weekend to visit Lorna and Francis at Winterdown, but I wasn't going alone. Tina and Jimmy were coming as well. I wasn't sure why. Derek stayed at home. We all knew the baby was expected soon, but not necessarily that weekend. Before we left that Friday night, Derek declared, "If the baby is a girl, I'm leaving home."

Tina, Jimmy, and I walked to Three Bridges Railway Station in the newly fallen snow. I wore no coat, just a thick orange sweater. I thought the snow, which I had never seen before, was beautiful—a winter fairyland. We walked past the shopping parade, where there was a bakery, a newspaper shop with a post office, a sweet shop, a hairdresser, a hardware store, and a fish and chips shop. Back then, chips were fat and wrapped in newspaper. The print rubbed off, leaving our greasy fingers dark with ink, which we licked anyway. No one gave a thought to the dangers of the toxic ink.

I liked walking down to the Pound Hill shopping parade on my own. It was my job to buy the bread for the day when I wasn't at school. I didn't feel the cold and was happy to leave the house for a while. I still believed I was returning to St. Vincent, to my friends, the sea, and the sunshine, back to Mummy and Daddy,

whom I missed every minute of every day. I was lonely
for their care and attention. I remember that particular
Friday with Tina, and Jimmy felt different because of
the snow. We jumped, slid, and laughed all the way to
the station.

I don't remember much else about the weekend at
Winterdown, except for us three children playing in the
snow with the two younger children at the bottom of
the hill. I recall Francis toasting crumpets on the open
fire in Lorna's sitting room before we went to bed, the
butter dripping through our fingers onto the carefully
held beautiful china plates. Tired and happy, Tina,
Jimmy, and I returned to Crawley the following day.

Snow still covered the ground when we reached
Crawley. We now had a baby sister. Sophie was born
on Holy Saturday, the day before Easter. Derek had not
left home. Instead, he proudly told us, "She's more my
sister than yours. I've known her longer." We all laughed
because Derek had kept a bag of clothes ready by his
bedroom door for weeks.

We children were told Thea was fragile and had
to stay in bed. She'd lost a lot of blood during the
birth, and we needed to be quiet and helpful around
the house. We didn't return to school the following
week because it was the Easter holiday. It was a happy
week—the home was calm and peaceful. Everyone was
fascinated with the baby, especially me. It was a new
experience living with such a tiny human being in the
house. The snow melted a few days later. It would be a
long time before I enjoyed it again. The world as I knew
it was about to fall apart.

One evening, when the baby was only a few weeks old, I was sitting quietly by the fire in the living room with Don, having a cup of tea before bed. The rest of the children were already asleep. Thea was in the kitchen with the baby when Don suddenly announced, "Thea is your mother, you know."

I didn't know what to do or say. I jumped up and went to the kitchen to see Thea, but it didn't help much. She was shocked that Don had told me. I tried to be grown-up about this new development, especially when Thea and Don said I needed to keep this story a secret. I mustn't tell anyone, not even the children. Later, alone in my bedroom, I felt devastated, trapped, and too young to voice an opinion about what would happen to me. I wondered how long before I returned to St. Vincent to see Mummy and Daddy again. I wrote to Mummy and told her what Don had said and that I would always love her best.

Difficult conversations followed. I would not be going to France or sailing back across the Atlantic to St. Vincent. I'd continue to go to Winterdown on the weekends until the summer. After that, I would stay permanently with my birth mother and my half-siblings. Once again, I was pulled away from everything familiar and comfortable.

I did what Mummy had taught: "Actions speak louder than words," "The devil finds work for idle hands," and "Hard work never hurt anyone." I brushed off the pain and threw my energy into doing as many activities as possible. Neither Mummy nor I wrote as often as before, and neither of us referred to this incident again until she was nearly ninety when she said, "You were only ever on loan. You rightfully belonged to Thea."

Although I didn't realise it at the time, as a fourteen-year-old, less mature than my peers, this traumatic experience impacted me deeply and left any possibility of a relationship with Thea in shreds for years. Re-reading my childhood diaries, decades later, I noticed the entries grew sporadic after my sister's birth. Often, there were only single-line entries, many blotched and scratched out. I wrote, "Nothing in particular happened." For a while, the entries stopped. I became a shy, awkward, silent teenager with brooding, secretive eyes. Those more kindly acquainted with my feelings called them "deep," but Thea described me as "cold and deceitful."

1964
An Escape From Reality

On the last day of school before the summer break and our move into the corner house. There was an occurrence of missing money, which had traumatic results for me. We children came home from school to find Thea fuming and Don silent. When Thea came home on Thursday nights from the Girl Guides, she always placed her belongings—purse, jacket, money, and papers—on a platform over the stairwell.

Thea and Don made us kneel in front of them and pray that the money would be returned. Then, we were sent to our rooms. Tina and I whispered in our room, prayed about the theft, and wondered how we would be punished. I hadn't taken the money, and she said she hadn't either. We didn't get to talk to the boys. By the end of the evening, no one owned up to taking the money.

Thea questioned us one at a time, and I was the last one. She made me place my hand on an open Bible and swear I hadn't taken the money. With tears streaming down my face, I insisted I hadn't, making her angrier. In a burst of temper, she shouted, "Know this, child, if you never forget this day, you are guilty of sin in both my eyes and God's. Now get out of my sight." I ran from the room, climbed onto the top bunk, and, neither speaking nor answering Tina's questions, sobbed into my pillow. I had never been treated this way before.

Thea's reversal of Mummy's kindness followed

me for a long time, causing significant repercussions in my future. She was cold, hard to please, and seemed uninterested in me. She appeared to prefer the boys over us two older girls. I couldn't fawn over her as the other children did, nor accept her as my mother. I lost the will to try and fit in after that incident. Nothing I did ever seemed to please Thea. I felt she judged me and never listened to me. Thea was nothing like Mummy.

Before I left the next morning to meet Lorna and Francis in London, Thea handed me a letter. "Give this to Lorna when you arrive." She didn't tell me what the note was about, but I thought it was likely concerning the stolen money. I nodded and stuffed it into my bag, thinking I would decide when to give it to Lorna.

I met Lorna and Francis at Westminster Bridge on their boat—*Weirakei II*, moored beneath Westminster Bridge and Big Ben. I was excited to stay for a week and motor down the Thames. A young man named David was on board. He was like an adopted son to Lorna and Francis. He would have been the other adult on board the ship when we sailed back to St. Vincent. He was ten years older than me, and when he asked if I'd like to see the sights in London before we undocked the next morning. I replied, "Oh, yes, please."

I carry a fond memory of that time in my heart. I remember strolling along Birdcage Walk and going to Buckingham Palace, where we watched the changing of the guard. We walked through St. James Park, enjoying the birds, watched the pedalos and rowboats on the Serpentine in Hyde Park, and stopped by the statue of Peter Pan. We also stopped outside 10 Downing Street.

We walked along the Embankment and listened to an outdoor concert before crossing London Bridge to the South Bank, where all the artists and book stalls were. I was enthralled listening to David tell stories about the historic buildings along the route—it was a great adventure for me and bolstered my crushed feelings after the incident with Thea.

When we left Westminster Bridge on *Wairakei II*, we cruised down the Thames. We passed places with interesting names: Canary Wharf, Isle of Dogs, and Greenwich. We continued past Woolwich, where the Thames Barrier would eventually be built, the Royal Arsenal, and on to the Thames estuary and Leigh-on-Sea. I do not remember how long the trip took or what I did on board, but I know I enjoyed being on the deck. I might have asked a few questions about where we were going and what we went by, but mostly, I was quiet.

The best part of my time that week was while we were anchored in the estuary. David, Lorna, and I went out in the dinghy and spent the afternoon sailing and swimming in the shallow marshy waters. After dinner, David added a sail to the dinghy, and we went out again in the ebbing sunlight. It was magical.

David was the sweetest, kindest man I had met. He reminded me of a much older Ben. It was one of the special times during my first year in England—a welcome escape from the reality of life in my English home. David moved to Switzerland shortly afterwards to begin a career working on the rigging of big yachts.

Before I left the boat, I handed Lorna the letter

from Thea. I was afraid that if I had given it to Lorna on my arrival, it would ruin my time on *Wairakei II*. I knew I might get into trouble, but I didn't care. Lorna chastised me for not giving it to her earlier, but she didn't read the letter before I left.

I never heard anything about the letter or the money again. My actions probably made Thea think I was deceitful and sly, but I didn't care. I had not taken the money.

I didn't see David again for over ten years. By that time, I was married and had a small child. David worked the ropes backstage for the Geneva Theatre Company and was at the London Coliseum for the production of the ballet, *Giselle*.

A New Address

A few weeks later, we moved into a four-bedroom council corner house,* facing a green, half a dozen doors up the street from where I first lived.

Tina and Sophie, once she was old enough, slept in one of the upstairs bedrooms facing the street and the green. The boys, Derek and Jimmy, had the big room at the back of the house, and I had the small room in the back corner with a tiny window overlooking the garden. Thea and Don slept in the other large bedroom in the front of the house. Although I had my own room, the house still felt cramped and noisy after fourteen years of freedom in the Caribbean. This house would become a place of traumatic experiences for all of us.

*Low income, city-owned housing.

Now that Lorna and Francis were in France, I couldn't go to Winterdown. But Don took me to London on Sundays to his Army Cadet barracks. He was a volunteer adult instructor in Tulse Hill for a group of cadets in the Territorial Army (TA), part of the British Army Reserve. On these trips, we always stopped at his Auntie Maggie's home. I loved her and her budgie, who would get mad at her and chirp in a voice that sounded like Auntie Maggie's, "Go to bed, go to bed, that is enough for today."

Neighbours

In all small communities, there are oddball families. And while we don't remember everything about the people from our past, some leave us with a clear memory.

When I first lived in Crawley, a little girl named Bernice (or Bunny, as her mother called her) and her brother Wade lived with their parents in the house next to ours. Jimmy and Bunny were about six, and Wade was still a toddler. It became suspiciously quiet one day when Bunny and my brother were upstairs. Jimmy was found cutting and shampooing Bunny's hair. His efforts were not without problems; he had cut deep grooves into her head with a pair of dressmaker's scissors and shampooed it with toothpaste!

Wade was usually the one in trouble. I heard stories of a neighbour calling his mother and saying, "For God's sake, go get that child of yours off the roof before he kills himself or I have a heart attack." I also heard him begging his little friend to egg him on to smash a hole in the greenhouse windows. "Go on, Bobby, tell me to do it. Come on, Bobby, tell me to do it, please!"

Another little girl, a toddler, about two years old, lived in a corner house near the main street. About once a week, this little girl would give her mother the slip. I can still see and hear her today, naked, except for her red Wellington boots and her shriek when she turned and saw her mother in pursuit.

In our new house, we had elderly couples on each side of us. Those on the right, the Talbots, weren't particularly friendly. They often complained to Thea over our dividing hedge about one of us children, our dog, or the garden in general. No one in our family was tidy, in or out of the house.

Those on the left were Londoners and lovely. Mrs. Ridgeway loved to bake and often made us fruit pies or cakes for tea. When Thea and Don were not home, we were supposed to go to her house and wait for them to return. Eventually, I was given a back door key to our house.

From a toddler to a teenager, Sophie spent many afternoons at Mrs. Ridgeway's home. She enjoyed having special teas with her while watching television, something we did not have. One of the saddest things I remember was Mrs. Ridgeway's husband dying of a heart attack on Christmas morning. Before the funeral, I recollect seeing her son, only five or six years older than I, and his hair had turned completely grey.

Jackie, a single mother, lived two doors up on the left. She had two daughters, one in a wheelchair because of polio, and a couple of boys. I rarely played with children in the street, preferring my own company most of the time. Jackie often had afternoon gentlemen callers. Although I didn't understand, I was aware of a white teddy bear sitting in the front window. It was a signal of her availability while her children played outside. The following day, she baked cakes for her immediate neighbours, a gesture that kept them sweet.

Across the green, on the other side of the curved road, lived a man whom I don't remember except for his name—Gordon Bennett. "Gordon Bennett" is an English idiomatic phrase that expresses surprise, contempt, or outrage. We children thought it funny only because the adults did. Also, on that side of the road lived a leggy young girl who wore coloured bands in her long black hair and wore short, colourful clothes. Don referred to her as "Twiggy" or "dolly-bird." Others were less complimentary.

Family Friends

Fredel and Gretel, an older couple from Austria, were friends of Don's since the end of WWII. Fredel had been a British prisoner of war. I only re-member them coming to visit once or twice. They were funny and loved to perform a skit about a quaint char-acter. Fredel stood behind Gretel, put his arms into the jacket sleeves she had over her shoulders, and put his hands into black boots. Gretel was the town mayor, speaking in a loud, guttural voice and gesturing widely with her hands. Fredel occasionally stamped his boots to emphasise what Gretel said. Of course, we children didn't understand anything because she only spoke Austrian, but their antics were hysterical. Those were fun times that lightened the tension I often felt around the house.

There was another family friend whom we called Uncle Roy. He and Don were captains in the Territorial Army (TA). Roy could waggle his ears and eyebrows independently; he was a clown. He'd take a mundane item, like the base of the Christmas tree, and turn it into a game. Sometimes, he put on the fez he always carried with him, pushed his rimless glasses to the end of his nose, and strutted about, making demands of everyone. "You," he shouted, pointing at one of the children, "Fetch me . . ." and then he'd mentioned something weird. The child he picked would scuttle off to find the item and bring it back. Then he'd say, "No, that's not what I wanted. Are you a nincompoop?" The adults treated this as a hilarious game, which the younger children automatically enjoyed. I felt it was belittling and refused to join in. I watched from the corner of the room, realising I could use my shyness to my advantage.

Tickling was another popular game adults played with children. Of the five children in the household, I was a teenager and considered too old, and Sophie, a baby, was too young. It was inappropriate to have boys squirming around on the floor, leaving only my other sister, Tina, to be tickled. According to research I have done, it is now known that tickling can overwhelm the nervous system in children and cause sexual arousal.

Many other people frequented our home: those involved in the Girl Guide movement, the Duke of

Edinburgh's Award, and Don's Army Cadets. Two of those boys, Dudley and Allen, often visited at weekends. Dudley was a loud, boisterous, heavyweight kind of guy, most probably in his early twenties. Allen was quiet, shy, tall, and thin as a rake. I liked him best.

Don and Thea's frequent use of ribald humour always embarrassed me. "Why don't you make tea for us, Jane? Dudley can keep you company. Or maybe you prefer Allen?"

"It's ok. I can manage," I'd mumble, blushing beet red.

But often, before I got to the kitchen, Thea or Don would send one of the boys after me. If it was Allen, we'd both be embarrassed by the suggestive comments that insinuated that we were misbehaving sexually. "We know what you're doing."

We were only doing what we were asked to do: making tea. We did that quickly and quietly and returned to the living room with the tea. My face was always bright red, Allen's too. I was so embarrassed that I wanted to escape, but I knew it would be considered impolite if I left the room.

One weekend, when I was around sixteen, I remember Dudley becoming aroused by their innuendos. He grabbed me, forced my small body against the kitchen cupboards, and began kissing me and pushing his hand under my skirt. I felt revolted by his overtures. I shoved against him as hard as I could, ducked under his arm, rushed into the bathroom, and locked the door. I stayed there so long that eventually, Thea banged on the door. "What's wrong with you? Open the door at once and come out!"

"I can't. I have a tummy ache."

"You'd better go upstairs to bed then. We are going down to the pub for a while."

"Are you all going?" I asked.

"Don, the boys and I are. The kids will stay here. It's time for them to get ready for bed anyway."

"Ok, I'll go upstairs as soon as you all leave, good night." I never went to the kitchen with Dudley again. Before Thea or Don said anything, I'd ask my sister to help me bring in the tea.

Peter was another friend of Thea and Don's. On one of his visits, I was working on my Queen's Guide Award and planning a trip to a special parade in London for extra credit. Peter turned to Thea and Don and said, "Why don't I take Jane to a show, as she will be in London?"

"That's an excellent idea," Don exclaimed. "It will be a good education for her."

I wasn't sure what kind of education Don thought Peter would give me. He wasn't a person I particularly liked. He had small, piercing eyes (like a snake), white, clammy skin, and small, cherry-red lips. I didn't want to go, but Don said it would be rude not to accept Peter's offer.

Thankfully, I'd booked a room ahead of the event at the Guide Headquarters on Buckingham Palace Road. I don't remember the show, but I still remember his sweaty hands and feeling relieved when another couple joined us in the opera box that night. After the show, Peter wanted me to walk to his apartment for a nightcap and spend the night. I was only seventeen!

"I already have a room at the Guide Headquarters. I must hurry because curfew is in half an hour."

"Well, that is a shame. Why don't you call and say you've changed your mind?"

"I can't do that. It wouldn't be true."

Much later, I discovered Peter had wanted to take me to Paris for a weekend, and Thea and Don had told him it would be OK. What were they trying to do? Marry me off, or put me in the same position as Thea had been with me? Pregnant!

2022
Adverse Childhood Experiences

In 1990, Thea finally decided to tell me my father's name—Richard Stanley Nicholls. I was in my forties, married, had three children, and divorced. Thea had believed that one of her sisters had told me about my father and that I had named my son after him. She was surprised to know it wasn't true.

It was now a morning in 2022, and Sophie was calling. My mind was already awhirl with confusing and painful emotions. In the last week, I found my birth father on *myheritage.com*, discovered five generations on my paternal side, and found cousins as far-flung as New Zealand. I learnt about a half-sister, Kathryn Anne, born in 1958. All I knew was that she was seven years younger than me and lived on the East Coast of the United States. Initially, my sister and I had set up a time to discuss issues on the *myheritage.com* website—I had too many entries for the same person. As she helped me navigate the site—we started talking about our life growing up in Crawley.

Sophie didn't suffer the sexual abuse that affected the rest of us, but she said her father, Don, constantly ridiculed her and spoke to her as though she were stupid because she couldn't spell well. I believe Don, fluent in at least French and German, wanted his daughter to be bilingual, but I never understood why he didn't include the rest of the family. He only spoke French to Sophie, which created tense family dynamics. By the time she went to school at age five, she didn't speak much English, which classified her as below standard in reading, spelling, and spoken communication. She was bright and learnt quickly but, sadly, never spoke French again. I had already left home and was living and working elsewhere. I wondered if Don's ridicule might have been the beginning of her anger.

That day in 2022, we talked about her anger for the first time, especially when she was a teenager. I asked her where she thought it had originated from and was shocked when Sophie replied, "Mum." She continued, "Mum never asked me if I minded doing something for her, and she still doesn't. She tells me what she wants done and how I must do it. She thinks she is always right, and I feel I have no choice."

"Why did you move her closer to you, then?" I asked.

"Selfishness, I suppose. Mum always phoned in tears, claiming no one called her, the TV didn't work, or some other petty thing. It was a twenty-minute drive to get to her house to fix the problem, and if I'd had a drink that evening, I couldn't go. Now that she lives next door, I can pop over for a few minutes and go straight back home."

"Oh," I said. "But that has left you to do everything for Mum."

Sophie then began to talk about her siblings. "Christina rarely calls. Mum was in the hospital for a month, and she only called once. Derek was here for the other weekend with Mary and the children, and all he did was sleep. Of course, Mum only complains that she didn't get to talk with him. She also says, 'Poor boy, he needs his sleep.' Right, the golden boy! He leaves his ninety-three-year-old mother to cope with his two noisy children. Derek makes me so mad."

"What about James? Why doesn't he come down more?" I asked.

"It's those damn dogs of his," Sophie replied with a disgruntled laugh.

We continued to talk about Mum's anger. Then I told her about the incident of the stolen money that Thea had said I was guilty of taking and how it had affected me all these years. "Have you ever heard that story?"

"Dad probably took the money."

"What?" I gasped. "Why would he do that?"

"Because he was deceitful, sly, and a liar."

Sophie echoed the words my mother had used all those years ago. A wave of shock, understanding, and sadness ran through my body like electricity. I was cold and hot all at the same time. "That would explain why Don was silent that night," I said.

After Sophie and I hung up, an incredible freedom flowed through me. It had been almost sixty years since Thea accused me of the "crime." I finally felt vindicated.

1965
Ramsgate

Ramsgate is a seaside town in Kent, on the south-east coastline of England. Its name comes from an Anglo-Saxon word meaning "Raven's Cliff." It is possible that when the missionaries of St. Augustine landed on the coast in 597 AD, the white cliffs were full of black ravens. The town is also home to the shrine of St. Augustine.

During the 19th century, Ramsgate became one of the great seaports in South-East England, famous for its beautiful, white sandy beaches. The town also made a name for itself during WWII. In the 1930s, the Mayor of Ramsgate conceived the idea for a network of tunnels under the city. R.D. Brimmell, a borough engineer and surveyor for Ramsgate, designed and built a network of tunnels to provide shelter for up to 60,000 people during air raids. They were ready for use in June 1939. The harbour was one of the main assembly points for Operation Dynamo from Dunkirk. Ramsgate is also home to a small population of feral, rose-ringed parakeets, which some sources claim escaped from a trading ship sailing from British India in the 1800s.

In mid-June, after I found out that I would start work at the bakery in the local shopping parade the following weekend, I received a letter from Lorna inviting me to come and stay with her and Francis on *Wairakei II* while they were moored at Ramsgate. I was excited to have one more weekend with them before I began my job. I took that Friday afternoon off from school, caught the train from Three Bridges followed by a coach at 6:30 p.m. from Victoria, and arrived in Ramsgate at 9:15 p.m. It was a long yet beautiful journey through the rolling Sussex and Kent countryside, especially on a warm and sunny evening.

The next day, Lorna and I went shopping at the local marketplace in the quaint medieval town of Sandwich. Lorna told me the story of John Montagu, the 4th Earl of Sandwich. Because he was an avid gambler, he refused to leave the tables for his lunch. He ordered his valet "to bring his meat stuffed between two pieces of bread." The locals followed suit because he was an Earl, and the word "sandwich" was born. I thought it was a great story, and in keeping with local tradition, Lorna and I had a sandwich each for lunch. Afterwards, we went to the fairgrounds, which I loved. It was exciting, especially as I found sixpence. Later, I went for a swim. I wanted to get as much practise as possible for my upcoming competitions and distance swimming. Unfortunately, the water was cold, and I couldn't stay in for long. We woke on Sunday morning to a hot day, perfect for swimming, but Lorna insisted that we go to church first, which messed up my plans to swim.

I had joined Lorna and Francis at Ramsgate a few times in the past year and particularly enjoyed hiking along the cliff trails. After church and lunch, I spent the afternoon walking to Dumpton Gap. I liked the story Lorna told me about the early Anglo-Saxon people naming the area "Hraefnes Geat" (Raven's Gate), referencing a gap in the cliffs. I thought *this must be the place where those people first saw the ravens.* The walk made me feel happy and light in spirit. To keep that feeling of happiness, I decided to finish my afternoon by going to the harbour and viewing the ships before I caught the coach to Victoria Station.

I always enjoyed walking along the docks and looking at the ships that came into the harbour. Many ships were from international ports. I relished watching the sailors working on the boats and listening to them talk in their native languages, most of them unknown to me. I could pick up a little French and German because of Don, and I was thrilled when the sailors grinned and waved at me. It made me feel pretty. It was fun, and their smiles made me think of Ben from the *Parthenon*. While walking along those docks, I had a secret wish. I imagined seeing the face of my first love. However, I never saw any Geest boats at Ramsgate.

On this visit, I watched a ship called *LaLuna* leave the harbour, and noted later in my diary, "There is an ominous cold north wind blowing, and I wish I were sailing with her."

When I arrived at the corner house, there was no one to greet me. I found food in the kitchen and made myself supper. I did my homework at the dining table and studied for my exams the next day. Still, no one came home. Feeling lonely, I took a lovely hot bath and went to bed. I dreamt I was back home in Calliaqua, and Mummy and Daddy were only a wall away.

1964 -1968
Christmases at the Corner House

Writing about Christmases in the corner house is painful. I have few memories or written notes. A friend described it perfectly when she said, "It is like lancing a boil and letting out all the bad stuff before you can heal and move on."

All I remember of my first Christmas in England, eleven months after leaving my island home, was that it wasn't a happy day. It wasn't the same kind of "bad" as the time Daddy came home drunk and tripped over my mini Christmas tree. I'd screamed at him back then, "This is the worst Christmas ever! " But Mummy believed in never letting the sun go down on your anger. She let bygones be bygones and had sent me to fetch Daddy to the table.

That first Christmas, no one was drunk or disorderly, but tensions were high. There was no sparkle of joy, love, or laughter around the table. No one, not even the adults, seemed happy.

The following Christmas was much better. I now had a job at Littlewoods, a departmental store, working at a dress counter—I recorded that I sold sixty-eight dresses on Christmas Eve. This meant I had money and could buy presents for everyone. Uncle Roy came down to entertain us the weekend before. We all enjoyed his visits—we forgot our struggles. It may have been that year that he and Don, returning from Aldershot or Farnham, had slipped into the forest and cut a live tree.

When they arrived and took the tree off the car, it was too big to fit into the house. They cut a section off the bottom, which Roy used for dramatic hilarity. He tied a rope around one end of the cutoff piece and dragged it around the garden, saying, "Here, Fifi, here. Let's go walkies." Then Roy held the tree stump on his head, pretending to be a society lady wearing a flamboyant hat and talking in a high-pitched soprano voice. He sounded like he had marbles in his throat. Laughter rang through the room and out the French doors into the watery,* sunshiny day. Next, he put the branches around his waist and danced back into the house, doing the hula-hula.

In retrospect, I believe Roy's clownish behaviour covered a sadness that, in the long term, affected us all. His laughter hid a fear that none of us realised—being gay in the early '60s wasn't talked about in family circles.

I noted that I received a few gifts on Christmas Day that year. They may have been clothes, but I was happy. I also recorded that Thea was in a terrible temper on December 31st. Don had said something that upset her.

The New Year brought a great outing with Lorna, Francis, Tina, and Derek. We went to the Bertram Mills Circus at the Olympia Exhibition Centre in Kensington. This was the last year that the circus would be in London. There was no cage act anymore, but a pick-pocket act was top of the bill! The clowns walked

---

*A "watery sun" isn't a typical sun. The sun is playing a trick on you. In approximately forty minutes, the sky will burst, and you will be soaked to the skin.

around the Big Top amongst the audience, sitting on ringside seats. They picked the pockets of a few people before returning to the ring. Then, they requested the owners come forward to get their items back. It was an amazing and fun act, but I was glad they didn't take anything from me. I would have felt so embarrassed.

I don't remember if we had a tree in 1966, but I expect we did because we had a party at the house the week before Christmas. It was the highlight of my Christmas that year. I wrote that I received kisses from everyone. The most exciting was from Alan, an art student, who held my face gently and kissed me under the mistletoe.

In re-reading my diaries, the high points of all our lives in the corner house were when people came to visit us. There were Girl Guide or church functions. When Roy or the two Army Cadets, Allen, and Dudley, came down any time of the year, but especially at Christmas, life had an upturn for us children. The care and energy Thea and Don expended for local youth in Girl Guides, the Duke of Edinburgh's Award, the Army Cadets in London, and later the Girls Venture Corps (GVC) left nothing over for their children. A person I still know from that period told me recently, "We got a lot from your Mum, but at the expense of you children."

Looking back, my siblings and I will never know why our mother or Don treated us the way they did because, as fragile human beings, it is hard to talk honestly to family members. Fear puts us in fight-or-flight mode, and trauma mushrooms from that process. Our mother had five children, ranging in age from an infant to teenagers, and our stepfather could never keep money in his pocket. The truth may set us free, but it is an uphill struggle to get to that point, and my mother has not been able to follow that path comfortably, even now.

My youngest sister remembers being given one of the "real" candles from the tree on Christmas Eve. Don lit it, and she carried it up the stairs to bed. As she walked, she sang a Christmas carol. The one she remembers is "Away in the Manger." I do not recall any lighted candles, probably because I had already left home. We both loved Midnight Mass on Christmas Eve. My memory was at St. Barnabas Church in Pound Hill. Sophie's memory is at the beautiful old Saxon church in Worth. My brothers were choir boys there until their voices broke.

I do remember Sunday services at Worth Church. I loved the high church rituals and the hymns. In 1968, I still lived at the corner house. I worked a full-time job and filled most evenings with Guides and Brownies. I spent weekends with my boyfriend, William. We went to the cinema on Saturday evenings in Redhill, and on Sundays, I usually went to dinner with his family. I was rarely at my house. Family events were non-existent. Two of my siblings were also teenagers and rarely at home. Although I have no written records for that year, I most probably spent Christmas at my boyfriend's house. Theirs was always a wonderful family affair with lovely food and lots of fun.

Memories from holidays, birthdays, and weddings tend to make or break a family. Having happy memories around children and the home are the ones that bring and keep families together. It isn't always the gifts we remember, but a joy shared. I believe that's why I remember my first fourteen years so vividly, living with Mummy and Daddy in the Caribbean.

1964 - 1968
Keeping Busy

I was still fourteen when Don gave me my Duke of Edinburgh's Award scheme booklet in August 1964. I am not sure whether he started me on the programme because he saw me as a troubled teenager or because he felt sorry for me.

After the money incident and our move to the corner house, I put my head down, did my schoolwork, asked no questions of my so-called parents, and spoke very little to my siblings. Christmas was nothing like it had been in the Caribbean. In England, at least one child was in tears within a few hours.

A few weeks after Sophie was born in April, I joined the 2nd Pound Hill Girl Guide Company, run by Thea. I completed the Guide Tenderfoot test card and was enrolled in May. In November, I finished my 2nd Class test card. I continued to earn at least one badge per month afterwards. These activities helped keep my mind away from the emotional trauma I was in.

I didn't know of the possible involvement of Don in the incident with the money at the time, so I thought he was being kind to me when he bought me the pretty new dress at the end of summer 1964. I loved it because

I'd only ever had cut-downs from Mummy's dresses. I enjoyed helping at the Army Cadet Force (ACF) canteen on Sundays. I was enthralled by the boys who paid attention to me. It was also a respite from the rest of the household, and I liked having something to do on weekends as I couldn't be with Lorna and Francis. Working in the canteen, I met Jim Enness.

New Year's Day in 1965 was fun. I spent it with friends from the 2nd Pound Hill Girl Guides. We first went to the headquarters in London, and then we spent some time feeding the pigeons in Trafalgar Square. I left London separately from the other girls. They went to Crawley, and I caught a train to Richmond to visit Anne. I still considered her my favourite older sister, even though she was my aunt. She had recently come to England from Tortola, in the British Virgin Islands, with her children, Bruce and Jeanne-Marie, whom I hadn't seen since I was nine. I had supper with the children and spent the night. It was nice to see Anne and Bruce, but Jeanne-Marie, who had epilepsy, was sometimes unpredictable. I worried she would have a Grand Mal seisure, fall, and hurt either herself or me.

I returned to school the next day, determined to be involved in as many activities as possible. I could already swim, but the school rules meant I had to achieve a certain level before I joined the Amateur Swimming Association team. Just before the end of January 1965, I took my first swimming test and the Bronze Personal Swimming Challenge. By March, I had completed the Silver and Gold proficiency tests and was in the youth championships with the Girl Guides. In June, I achieved the two-mile distance swim, the highest a girl could attain at my school. There were still classes, tests, and homework every night. I helped at a Girl Guide and Brownie Pack and babysat for a family with three little children once a week. Plus, I made most of my dresses from Simplicity patterns in my spare time.

I completed my Duke of Edinburgh's Award Bronze Expedition in February of 1965 by marching fifteen miles overnight with the Army Cadets from the ACF headquarters in Tulsa Hill to Winterdown. We left London at midnight and arrived at Winterdown at 08:15 hours. The cadets teased me that I walked three times as far because I took three steps to every one of theirs! I completed a nature study of the plants and animals later that morning before returning to Crawley.

In June, I applied and got a job at the bakery in the Pound Hill Parade on Saturday mornings. I earned ten shillings a pay packet. There was a Girl Guide trip to Meschede, Germany, in August, and I needed to make more money than the troop-organized jumble (yard) sale totals of £25, which would be divided among the three girls chosen to go on the trip.

At the end of July, Tina, Bruce, and I took the ferry to Calais and the train to Paris to meet Lorna and Francis on Wairakei II. We spent a wonderful summer holiday in Paris. In August, I left Crawley for the Girl Guide's ten-day trip to Meschede.

All other entries in my diary for 1965 were filled with school activities, especially chemistry, which I liked but never did well in. I sat at the back of the class and rarely got the teacher to help me. I was unpopular in class when, during an experiment, I added the wrong substances to the test tube, and the liquid exploded in the sink. Because the correct care of chemicals was never explained to me, I would have a similar accident later working for Philips in Salfords.

By September, I'd completed my Bronze Duke of Edinburgh Award, and by November, I had received thirteen proficiency badges in the Girl Guides. With this achievement, I could leave Thea's Guide Company and train to become a cadet. In my final week as a Girl Guide, I got to carry the Union Jack at the church parade on Sunday. I had wanted to be chosen for a while, but Thea had kept telling me I wasn't ready.

I started my Girl Guide cadet training in January 1966 while still in school. At sixteen, I learnt to play badminton. I also completed an extensive paper for a section of my Silver Duke of Edinburgh Award called Design for Living. The topic, "My House," covered all aspects of how to buy, design, and furnish a home. I received my award in January 1967, my last year at Hazelwick. I took my General Certificate of Education (GCE) exams in four subjects and left school in August. I wanted to train as a nurse and go overseas, but it wasn't meant to be. What I wanted and what the careers office thought I wanted conflicted, and Thea and Don wanted me to get a job to contribute to the household income.

With no means to independently pay for an education, I was at the whim of Thea and Don. He arranged a job for me at Mullard (M.E.L.) on the Crawley Industrial Estate, where he worked. I hated the job. I worked on the shop floor in a big factory, almost causing a "walk-out." I'd dared to open a window in the ceiling without asking permission from the Union. Less than a year later, I transferred to the Philips Electronic Laboratory in Salfords. There, I worked in a "clean lab," producing the first integrated circuits.

I still lived at home in Pound Hill, cycling twelve miles a day to and from work. I now spent three evenings a week working with two Girl Guides and a Brownie Company. I still babysat one night and went out with William for one or two nights. I finished my cadet training and became an Assistant Guider in August 1968, starting my own company at Hazelwick School in February 1969. By the age of nineteen, I was rarely home.

1965
A Day in the City—Never to be Forgotten

It was a cold, grey winter morning when I met Lorna at Victoria Station at 10:00 a.m. on January 30th. We were there to observe Winston Churchill's funeral. I could hear Big Ben's distinctive chimes echo through the silence of the London streets. We saw the royal family leave in their coaches before moving on to St. Paul's Cathedral, where we watched the procession of the coffin weaved through the streets. Churchill was the first civilian of the 20th century to be granted the honour of a state funeral, usually reserved only for kings and queens.

The streets were crowded with people of all kinds, some openly weeping, while others took advantage of the situation because we were packed so tightly. I felt a hand crawling under my skirt and stepped back heavily on the foot of the person pressed closely behind me. The hand moved away.

I had watched a couple of funerals as a child in St. Vincent. They were very different, and none were for dignitaries. For those I watched, the women dressed in white, and followed the coffin wailing loudly.

The pomp and ceremony of Churchill's funeral awed me. I read later that an estimated 350 million people watched the service on television. Military bands played dirges and somber marches as Churchill's coffin, draped with the Union Jack, moved through the streets of London borne by men from the services of nearly twenty different military units. I was just one of approximately one million people who lined the streets that day. The British like to say farewell to their famous people in style. Even I, who had lived a simple, naive life in the Caribbean, had read about the famous man who defended Great Britain from the Nazis in WWII. "England will never be the same again," Lorna said with a sigh.

I must have gone to Chartwell, the home of Winston Churchill for over forty years, the following year when it first opened to the public because I wrote a short poem that year.

> *A willow*
> *tree*
> *weeps over*
> *Chartwell pond.*
> *I heard a*

whisper
in the wind,
time passes
great men
die.

With the procession over, Lorna and I made our way, in the opposite direction of the crowds, to the Lyons Corner House Cafe on Coventry Street, Piccadilly. We ordered tea and a light lunch of delicate, delicious white bread sandwiches—crusts removed—filled with smoked salmon topped with watercress. Afterwards, Lorna and I went to Madame Tussauds for the afternoon. I thought it incredible how lifelike the wax figures were. The tableau I remember the most was Sleeping Beauty. Her chest went up and down, making it look like she was breathing. Lorna let me go down to the dungeons, where I was fascinated by the gruesome characters and stories of their crimes.

Lorna and I caught the train back to Winterdown from Victoria Station around 5:00 p.m., arriving back at the house in a taxi from Esher to the end of the driveway. We walked up the long path in the dark on that cold wintry night. At least it didn't snow that day.

I slept well after another lovely meal with Lorna and Francis. The next day, Don came to pick me up. I was going with him to the army barracks in London to help serve the cadets tea and biscuits in the canteen for the first time. It was great fun. After the meeting was over, we drove back to Crawley. It had been a wonderful, action-filled weekend. My imagination raced with everything I had experienced.

1965
Holiday in Paris

At the beginning of the school summer holidays in 1965, I took my sister, Tina, and my cousin Bruce on the train to France. We were meeting Lorna and Francis in Paris. Tina and Bruce were nine and seven years of age. I am surprised looking back that at fifteen and only being in England for eighteen months, I was solely responsible for two younger children on a long and complicated journey.

The week leading up to our trip was wet. Notes in my diary showed that I participated in the town sports events and won the Swimming Shield trophy for Hazelwick School. I watched a cricket match between the teachers and the boys with the rest of the third and fourth-year classes, and we got caught in a thunderburst and had to run for cover.

Don took Tina, Bruce, and me to Newhaven, near Brighton, on the South coast of England, to start our journey to Paris. We three children boarded the ferry crossing the English Channel at 11:45 a.m. We arrived in Dieppe four hours later and boarded a steam train. It took another two to three hours before we arrived in Paris, where Francis met us at Saint Lazare train station. It was a long journey, and we were tired.

After a good night's sleep, Francis took us around the Eiffel Tower gardens, which were beautiful. I loved the formality, and the fountain was incredible. Bruce and Tina enjoyed running up and down the pathways between the trimmed hedges. Going up the Eiffel Tower was scary. I was the only one who went to the top, although I never let go of the rails. The tower stood 984 feet high, and the sway of all that metal at the top was terrifying.* I thought about a story I'd heard: if someone dropped a pea from the top, its speed and velocity would break the pavement below or split a man's head open. I didn't want to fall or drop anything.

The next day, Francis motored *Wairakei II* through the canals to Poincy, a community on the River Seine/Marne, where we stayed for a few days.

It took us over seven hours, but it was a marvellous journey. Lorna prepared all our meals and showed us how to work the locks. We also walked along the canals, swam, sat on the deck, and watched the French countryside go by. It was a relaxing diversion from being at home. I was happy that Tina had begged to come on this trip with me, and Anne had let Bruce come too.

The next day, we all went to Meaux, a local marketplace; unfortunately, it was closed. Back at the boat, Francis suggested we children might like to take the dinghy out and have fun because Lorna, who had a headache, wanted "a little peace and quiet."

Francis swung the davits out over the port side of *Wairakei II* and lowered the little boat into the water. He held the painter while we children climbed in, then Francis stepped in, took a seat in the centre of the small boat, and rowed us up the canal to a place where the

---

*Gustave Eiffel used latticed wrought iron to construct the tower to demonstrate that the metal could be as strong as stone while being lighter.

trees along the towpath hung over the water. It was pretty and cool in the scorching August sun. Once there, he handed me the oars and said, "Your turn." I had never rowed before, but Francis gave me a quick lesson and watched me for a while before directing me to pull up to a couple of steps coming off the towpath. He jumped out of the dinghy, saying, "OK, kids, have fun. I'm going to walk back."

I was strong and enjoyed the thrill of pulling the oars together and skimming through the water as I rowed away from the bank while the other two waved goodbye. We had fun for about an hour, paddling back and forth across the river, but my arms eventually tired. I caught a crab (made a mistake) with the right oar and lost control. The oar lifted out of the rowlock** and went overboard. For a split second, I stared at the oar floating in the water. Then I turned my head and said, "Stay in the boat while I get the oar." I did not stop to think about the possible dangers—the tide or pollution. I just dove in and swam towards the oar.

As I swam, I realised the tide was taking the oar further away from me. I swam faster, reached it, and turned around. The current was against me now, and the oar was cumbersome. It felt like the dinghy was separated from me by a large expanse of water. In reality, the distance was probably only about ten or fifteen feet, but my mind whirled, and panic set in. What if I couldn't reach the dinghy, and it floated past with the children? It would be my fault if I didn't get there in

** A swiveling device attached to the gunwale of a boat that holds an oar in place and acts as a fulcrum during rowing.

time. The boat with Tina and Bruce would float away and be lost.

I was afraid for a few seconds. Then I remembered that when I lived in St. Vincent, I swam to Youngs Island and walked through the sea urchins under the ocean swells. This was nothing, I told myself. I was more than capable of getting back to the boat.

As I neared the dinghy, I shouted at Bruce to use the other oar and scull as hard as he could towards me. "I made it," I shouted. "Bruce, drag your oar into the boat. Don't let it fall in. Tina, can you take this oar from me, please?"

I cried out again as they leaned out on my side to help me back in. "Don't try to pull me in—you might capsize the boat. I'll hang here for a bit and then get in. Everything's good now," I gasped. "We are all together."

We floated as I rested before hauling myself up with a strong pull and flopping into the boat. "Phew, I made it!"

We were silent for a moment before I said, "I don't think we should tell Lorna about this. Her headache might worsen." Everyone laughed, recalling the story of Francis saying, "H..l begins with Lorna." I added, "If she asks, I'll say I jumped in the water because I was hot."

"Did you have a good time? Are you all hungry?" Lorna asked when we returned.

"Yes!" We replied in unison.

We ate the lunch Lorna prepared without further talking, then lay on the stern deck on towels and enjoyed the sun's warmth. I learnt later that swimming in the rivers and canals had been outlawed since 1923, and one was fined if caught. I don't remember taking the dinghy out again on that summer holiday in France, nor do I remember if we ever told any of the other grown-ups. I'm sure I would have recalled if Thea had known. She probably would've let me forget.

The day before our return to Paris, we walked along the canal in the pouring rain to a farmhouse in Trilport to buy eggs and bread. I looked through the open kitchen door and saw a long wooden table with many people sitting around it. It looked like they were eating bread and cheese and drinking wine, even a girl who appeared to be about four years old. Much to Lorna's disgust, I took off my shoes on our way back to the boat, preferring the wet grass on my feet to slippery, damp shoes.

The following morning, we were up at 6:30 a.m., ready for the taxi to take the three of us back to St. Lazare Station. Crossing the English Channel was lovely, the weather mild and the sea smooth. Thea, Don, Jimmy, Sophie, Anne, Jeanne-Marie, and Anne's lifelong friends, Marn and Gordon Beedell met us in Newhaven. It was a happy family reunion. There was never another trip as fun as that summer's vacation in Paris.

1965
Meschede, Germany

Theresa, Barbara, and I were the three girls chosen from our Girl Guide company to go to Meschede, Germany. We first met Miss Stromwall, the group leader from our area, in Brighton the week after our big jumble sale in July 1965. The sale raised £25, equivalent to just under £460 in today's currency. In a letter, she stated:

> *I have already met Frau Rode, who is*
> *arranging hospitality in Meschede. She hopes,*
> *that in the evenings, we will get together as*
> *a party with the German girls, for Campfire*
> *singing, folk dancing, and miming.*

In Brighton, Miss Stromwall emphasised that we remember our motto: "We must BE PREPARED." We learnt a few German phrases, camp songs, and some dances: *Circassian Circle*, *Haste to the Wedding*, and the *Cumberland Long Eight*. These are all folk dances of Scottish origin and part of the repertoire of the British Isles and North American fiddle traditions. Today, I can't recall if I participated in those dances, but I was grateful I didn't play an instrument. The idea of performing in public was intimidating.

Miss Stromwall also wrote about the town where we would be staying: In her words:

> *Meschede is a small country town surrounded*
> *by wooded hills in the Ruhr Valley, similar*
> *to Lancashire and Yorkshire. The population*
> *is young. After the war, the town took many*
> *East German refugees who have become quite*
> *assimilated. There are good shops and a typical*
> *German dance hall run by Catholics, which*
> *ensures control. There is also a Protestant*
> *Church. The chief recreation is walking through*
> *wooded valleys. But there is no doubt at*
> *all, hospitality is a great feature of the West*
> *Germans.*

Miss Stromwell also said that each girl would stay with a different host family and meet up with the other twelve Guides and German girls during the days and evenings. My diary notes say that while excited about the trip, I was more worried about not hearing from the Army Cadet, Jim Enness, with whom I thought I was in love.

My name was put on a free collective passport because purchasing an individual passport cost thirty shillings. We had to travel in full uniform, with a Union Jack badge sewn onto the sleeve, which cost sixpence. On our return to England, we'd exchange it for a world flag badge, which was exciting; I would sew it onto my camp blanket with my other badges. The list from Miss Stromwell continued:

> *Uniforms will be worn when we go out*
> *officially, but on other occasions, Mufti will*

*be worn. A camp uniform is optional, get into
training, as the area is a first-rate walking
country. I suggest as a gift to your hostess, you
take either a tin of Nescafe (2oz), a 1/4lb
of tea, or possibly a drying-up cloth with
a typically English design. Please fill the
enclosed three pages with postcards, brochures
and something interesting from your town.
Remember, they are foreigners, and you must
write very clearly.*

I bought a linen tea cloth for my hostess with a print of St. John's Church and the town square in Crawley, and for her daughter, Dorothea, I bought English chocolate. We were told what to pack. Nothing was left to our imagination. Everything we took had to go into a light suitcase or duffle bag and a haversack,* but no rucksacks (backpacks). I imagine Don loaned me a haversack from the Army Cadet unit, and Thea loaned me a small suitcase. I packed a sandwich tin, thermos, the greaseproof paper we were asked to bring, and my overnight things into the haversack.

*Your kit list must include:
Plimsolls** for country dancing.
Plastic Macintosh and hood.*

---

*The word haversack is an adaptation of the German Hafersack and the Dutch haverzak, meaning "oat sack." A small cloth bag on a strap worn over one shoulder, originally the bag of oats carried for the horses. The term havresac was adopted by the English and French cavalries in the seventeenth century.

** A low, canvas lace-up shoe.

Night things and slippers.
Change of underclothing and sanitary towels.
Washing kit, including soap and towel.
Hairbrush and comb.
Writing material. Songbook.
Sunglasses. Clothes brush.
Mending outfit, shoe cleaning kit, and badge
polish.
Jeans or slacks and shirt, cardigan or sweater.
Summer dress or skirt and blouses.

Because the Dover ferry to the continent left at
9:00 a.m., we were asked to arrive the evening before
and to bring an extra blanket; we would spend the night
"camping" in Hastings Hall.

Mattresses and pillows are provided. Our
supper will be at 6:00 pm, then we can have
the evening together to practise our songs and
dances and to make our plans.

On the afternoon of the August 23rd, Theresa,
Barbara, and I met at our local church, St. Barnabas.
The press was there to interview us before Mr. Doughty,
Theresa's dad, drove us down to Hastings. We must have
scrambled to get to the ferry on time the next day, as my
diary states that I woke up at 8:30 a.m., and the ferry
left promptly at 9:00 a.m.

Food was paramount in my early years. We didn't
get given our packed lunches on the ferry. When we
finally got to Köln, Germany, eight hours later, I was

famished, which is why I never forgot our supper in the youth hostel that night—a watery brown soup with a few vegetables and a long sausage shaped like a horseshoe, floating in the liquid. Any food would have been adequate, but it didn't look good.

Theresa, Barbara, and I spent three hours the following day exploring the city. I was fascinated by the cathedral; it was incredibly ornate and beautiful. It is astounding that during WWII, the city of Köln was bombed to the ground by the British Royal Air Force (RAF), yet the cathedral remained standing.*** Later, we gathered at the railway station for an overnight train to Meschede.

Tired and rumpled, our leaders paired us with our host families. My host family lived in town, but Theresa's family lived further out on a farm. Dorothea, the daughter of my host family, was two years younger than me but seemed far more sophisticated. I was tongue-tied by my self-consciousness. I knew I would miss being in close contact with Theresa. I was also envious of her being with the good-looking boy, Hans, on the farm.

We spent the day meeting all the German hostesses and their families and finished with a social at the local church in the evening. When Dorothea and I arrived at her home that night, I was happy to climb the stairs to my tiny loft bedroom and go to bed. I fell asleep instantly between the two gigantic, over-stuffed feather duvets.

***The city of Köln (Cologne) was bombed in 262 separate air raids by the Allies during World War II, all by the Royal Air Force. The RAF dropped 34,711 tons of bombs on the city.

The room only contained a bed; there was no space for a chair or table. Writing letters home, which I did every day, was difficult. I couldn't sit on the bed without being folded into the middle of cotton and feathers, and I spilt my ink on the beautiful, pristine white covers. I tried to get it out but only spread the stain further across the duvet, which made me uncomfortable and nervous. Still, I wrote my letters. Three to Jim, babbling on about everything I had done over the last few days. Two to Mummy and Daddy and a couple more letters to Thea, Don, and my siblings.

I loved the sites we visited: the Klause—an old hermitage in the hills. The small village of Eversberg, with its ruins, on which we could climb to the top. There were many beautiful old buildings and quaint cottages. I could feel the history in those buildings. In contrast, the Benedictine Abbey was modern with its odd angular shape.

We had at least three social gatherings at the dance hall, for folk dancing and campfire singing, with the host families and the twelve other girls from England. I did attempt the *Cumberland Long Eight*; it was the simplest. But then I retreated to the back wall with Theresa, who was awkward like me, to avoid being included in other dances. Dorothea was very good at dancing. I was happy to watch her and the other German girls and boys twirling and spinning around the room in their traditional dirndls. The campfire singing was different; I sang with gusto, loving every minute, not caring if I wasn't always in tune.

I was upset to find the post office closed on

Saturday. I wanted to get my last letters to Jim and the corner house in the mailbox. But I soon forgot my disappointment when we boarded a boat trip around Hennessee Lake.

I don't remember seeing Dorothea's mother smile once, but she loved to cook. I wrote in my diary, *We had a wacking big dinner, with cake and coffee to follow at 2:00 p.m.* I didn't write about the pink blancmange I couldn't swallow. But I recall it tasted of fresh strawberries. I was so embarrassed because my throat constricted, and I couldn't swallow. I had to rush from the table and be sick. Later, Dorothea and I went to a fair; the roller coaster was my favourite ride. There was a big party for everyone on the afternoon of our last day.

I had to be up at 5:00 a.m. for the taxi to get me to the rail station. Nearly all the teenagers and host parents came to wish us goodbye. There was a lot of hugging, waving, and promises of letters as we gathered at the station. I never forgot one of the phrases I learnt: *Ich bin Phadfinderinnen*, I am a Girl Guide. I loved the sound of the words rolling off my tongue.

We were bound for Remagen and a riverboat ride to Koblenz. Once there, we visited the zoo and spent the night in a hostel near the river. The next morning, we visited the historic Basilica of St. Castor, where Miss Stromwell advised us to take special notice of the recently restored organ. However, most of the girls were interested in the gift shop. The rest of the day was ours to explore, and we were allowed to wander at will. We met again to have a meal before boarding our train to Calais. That night, the ferry crossing was rough, making us late into Dover.

When we finally arrived at Hastings Hall, Don waited impatiently to take us home. He was angry. *Damn*, I thought, *we're home*. I ran into the building, picked up our extra blankets, and left quickly. There was no time to say farewell to the other twelve girls. Don drove in silence, which allowed us to sleep all the way home, keep our memories intact, and avoid Don's temper.

1965 - 1967
School Lunches

For the first two years of living with Thea and Don, I felt untethered, foreign in England, the place of my birth, with my actual mother and my four siblings. My soul still languished thousands of miles away in the Caribbean with Mummy and Daddy.

School lunches were the only times I felt part of the teenage world around me. Usually, I would eat quietly and listen. I wasn't popular. I believed I was considered a bit of a nerd, but I could always be counted on to go through with an idea if it appealed to my sense of humour. Or if I said I would.

There were always stories and tidbits of teenage girl information to learn at the dining tables. Who was wearing stockings? Who had started their period? Who had siblings at home, those "cute little darlings," and those at school, whom they vehemently shunned until they had to walk home with them after classes. Even then, the younger children walked behind their older brothers and sisters until they reached the bridge.

The railway bridge, built years ago to carry the tracks to London, was the right of passage from school to home and vice versa in the mornings. It was a no man's land, where, by some unspoken code, the school world no longer existed, and kids were different once they passed under it. I never had that problem or pleasure, as my siblings were more comfortable with their peers than I was and were more likely to shun me than the other way around.

Four or five "dinner ladies" reigned supreme over what we ate each day of the week. Boys and girls did not sit together at a table back then but were segregated by age and sex. Once placed at a table, you were there for the school term. Instinctively, I knew it was best to be quiet and not voice an opinion.

Each day of the week was a different meal. It always included meat, potatoes, and two vegetables, followed by a cake dessert baked in large tin trays and served with custard; everything was cooked in the kitchen behind the serving hatch. A runny brown and red minced beef stew was served every Tuesday, topped with mashed potatoes, a thin crust of cheese, and tinned peas and corn. On one of those Tuesdays, a girl chose to describe, in graphic detail, her cat having kittens. It was gruesome, and remembering her story that day, my stomach turns briefly sour as I write. I was the only one who finished my lunch, gaining the grudging admiration of the other girls at the table. I saw it only as tasty food.

I ate without looking at the plate. I knew Mummy's admonishment: "To leave food on your plate is a wickedness close to uncleanliness when there are people worse off than you." Back home in the Caribbean, Mummy would never let me leave the table before clearing my plate, and believe me, liver was worse than the runny stew. My lessons had been well learnt. I ate everything not from a sense of pride but a sense of honour for the person I loved and missed dearly.

School lunches cost a shilling. Several different coins equalled that coin: two six-penny pieces, four three-penny pieces, six tuppenny pieces, and twelve pennies. There were still twelve pennies to a shilling in the 1960s. It was another thing that was difficult to learn. In St. Vincent, we used a hundred pennies to the dollar. In England, the decimal system didn't come into effect until 1971.

We sat ten to a table with approximately twenty tables in the room. One of the dinner ladies was a fastidious, large woman. She did not appear to like us. Perhaps it was just teenagers she disliked. She would take a long time to pick up our shillings or equivalent coins and put them in the small brown envelope she carried for each table. Only after she had sealed the envelope, were we allowed to line up for our dinner.

We decided to pay her back for her disdain. One day, we agreed we would each bring in twelve pennies instead of the regular shilling or two sixpences kids usually brought each day. A British penny was a large coin, bigger than a shilling, and larger than an American quarter. The dinner lady insisted on counting each pile, penny by penny. If she dropped a coin, she would start over. A slight bump from underneath the table assisted nicely with our little drama.

Word got around about what we planned to do, and a few more tables participated. It didn't take long for the room to become a cacophony of sniggers, coughs, and table-thumping. Lunch was delayed because of our actions that day, and I don't remember eating the main course—cold, fat-congealed meat—but I do recall eating the dessert, chocolate cake with pink custard.

There was no playground time for anyone that day, and a few children were late to our English afternoon class. I remember one boy's answer to the teacher. "It wasn't my fault, sir; the dinner lady wouldn't let us get our dinner."

"And why was that, young man?"

"She kept dropping the dinner money, Sir."

No one laughed. We risked the double-ruler whack across the back of our hands if we did. I don't remember anyone getting into trouble over the incident, but for the next week, the headmaster took up a position at the back of the dining hall. Our actions brought change. We were divided into two lines entering the dining hall, boys in one line and girls in the other, and made to sit five boys and five girls at each table. It was a quiet week. Things did get back to normal with two exceptions: we were no longer segregated, and we had a different dinner lady to collect our money.

In my Fifth year at Hazelwick, I no longer ate lunch in the dining hall. I would go to the student centre next to the new Upper Fifth building and hang out during lunch. In a family of five children, pocket money (allowance) was sporadic. Instead of having lunch, I'd take three pennies from my shilling and buy a wagon wheel biscuit—two thin cookies sandwiched with marshmallow cream and covered with chocolate. Occasionally, I bought two. Milk was still free to students in 1967. If I went straight to the student hall at the end of class, I could get three small bottles, equivalent to one pint.

The following year, I moved into the Upper Fifth part of the school, where I met quite a few people who became my friends. Linda, who was new to the area, was my best friend for many years, as well as William, who became my boyfriend, and Graham, his best friend. Thea and Don wanted me to leave school at sixteen to bring in extra cash. Fortunately, the headmaster persuaded them that it would be beneficial for me socially to stay on another year. I was grateful that they agreed, as it was my best year of school in Crawley.

The Upper Fifth had a separate dining room where the teachers, prefects, and Upper Fifth students ate. It was also used as the assembly hall. It had large windows looking out onto the fields and woods beyond. We had polished round tables with seating for six people. I have no memory of having lunch in this building because I continued to go to the student lounge and, if I was lucky, get the free milk to go with my wagon wheel biscuits.

It was about this time that pantyhose became popular. Stockings had never been a hit with me. I loathed the feel of those dangling fasteners attached to the stockings, which would twist and pull within a short time of wearing. Maybe if I could have afforded silk ones, I wouldn't have minded them as much. I couldn't imagine why a contraption like the suspender belt ever became popular.

I saved the nine pennies left from my daily lunch money to buy pantyhose. If I was diligent, I could buy a new pair every other week and still save some money for other things. This wasn't too difficult—I didn't socialise with other teenagers or wear makeup. I was raised by Mummy, who didn't believe in frills and trimmings. Her mantras were "Pride goes before a fall," "Pretty is as pretty does," and "Only those born with a silver spoon in their mouth can afford to have trimmings."

I learnt to take care of myself to survive the roiling emotions still in my head. I hated to ask Thea for money to buy feminine pads. It was embarrassing.

Rebellion Begins

Following the school lunch disturbance, a few girls included me in their circle. I do not believe they were the best company to keep, but I was happy to have found anyone willing to talk to me, walk home with me, and even pass a few notes in class. One day, one of the girls asked if I would like to have lunch with them off the school premises. I agreed, thinking we would get back in time for the afternoon class. That was not the girls' idea. Skipping school terrified me—I was afraid my absconding from school would get back to Thea and Don. It was so terrifying that I never did it again. It put me back into the nerd crowd, but I had made one friend, Susan, from that group outing.

Susan, who was in the "C" stream at school, hated the wasted time she spent in the common room playing board games. She complained bitterly that her teachers wouldn't help her when she asked. "They won't give me a chance. They act as if I'm ignorant," She said.

There was no help for children who were either slow learners or didn't fit the school requirements for attendance back then. Susan told me her teachers said, "We're too busy to teach one child differently from the rest."

I tried to talk to Thea about how unfair Susan's situation was, but she was dismissive. "What's the point?" she said. "You need to keep your head down and study."

One weekend, I sat at the dining room table trying to write an essay for my new English teacher, Mr. Frederick Turner—he gave me the creeps. The essay was titled "Joycing the Hemingway." The books we were working from were *Ulysses* and *A Farewell to Arms*. I disliked both books intensely, almost as much as I disliked Mr. Turner and Thea's attitude about my friend's educational dilemma.

Joyce's *Ulysses* was a stream-of-consciousness writing with minimal punctuation or capital letters. It was tiresome to read. I thought Hemingway's *A Farewell to Arms* was unhappy, and Mr. Turner, our teacher, wasn't a happy man either. He gave us impossible essays to write and was always disappointed by the results. Still upset with Thea's comments about Susan's predicament, I muttered, "If only Mr. Turner would help students like Susan and stop giving the rest of us ridiculous essays to write, a lot of children might be happier."

"You need to mind your own business, and don't talk like that about your teacher," Thea shouted through the dividing doors.

"I wish you'd just shut up," I said under my breath. I wasn't quiet enough because the next minute, Thea walloped me upside my head. It sent my ink pen sprawling across the page and clattering to the floor.

"Go to your room this instant!"

Later, I crept downstairs, retrieved my books and pen, and finished my essay, killing them both. The deaths were simple, concise, and straightforward, in the Hemingway style and the stream-of-consciousness Ulysses style. My essay was about my thoughts, while in the bath, before going to their funerals: Thea's and Mr. Turner's. I received a failed mark for my essay, not because of the subject matter, but for the ink blotch across the paper.

Another instance of rebellion happened when I was in my Fifth year at Hazlewick. It was 1966. I was still mostly quiet. My classmates barely noticed that I existed until one hot afternoon. It was our second year with Mr. Matt, our maths teacher. The previous year, he'd introduced himself to the class by walking in and saying, "I am a musician and a mathematician." He approached the blackboard and wrote: **My name is Mr. Matt, and I am not to be walked on.**

Most of the class laughed out loud, many behind his back for the rest of the year.

I remained quiet, thinking, *he's crazy*. He began the lesson that first day by playing his violin to explain that all music is math and vice versa. Unfortunately, his correlation between the Pythagorean theorem and music was lost on most of our "B" stream students. I struggled through that year, never quite making a good grade but getting a C+ for effort.

In the Fifth year, we were supposed to be learning calculus. I was, as Mummy would say, "Up a creek without a paddle!" I tried hard to understand, but everything I did in class made no sense when I walked out the door later. I was too shy and easily intimidated to ask my teacher for help. He usually set a problem for homework at the end of class, telling us, "Go home and figure it out."

There was a girl in my Fifth-year maths class whom I greatly admired. I didn't know her name. We wore school uniforms—gray skirts, white blouses, blue blazers, and blue and red ties—but she flaunted live flowers in her hair, no tie or blazer, and often no shoes or socks on her feet. She considered herself a member of the "Flower Power Movement." I envied her relaxed style, honeyed laugh, wide, mascaraed eyes, and loose, flying blonde hair. She embodied the freedom I wanted.

On that hot, stifling afternoon in June, locked in an airless classroom with twenty-nine other bodies, Mr. Matt droned on, dictating problems we were to work on over the weekend.

Suddenly the girl spoke up. "Sir, I don't understand... ."

"Be quiet," Mr. Matt interrupted.

"But Sir, I only— "

"Sit down and be quiet."

"But Sir —"

"You will write one hundred lines, girl: 'I will be quiet and listen.'"

"But Sir—"

"Another hundred lines! Add, 'I will not answer back.'"

At this point, I jumped out of my seat and shouted, "Stop! Stop giving her lines! She is only trying to ask you a question. Listen to her!" All heads swiveled in my direction.

A stunned silence followed before Mr. Matt thundered, "Come here at once!"

Internally quaking, more with fury than fear, I got up and walked to the front of the class. "You are wrong," I said when I reached his desk.

"How dare you challenge my authority!" he shouted. "We are going to see Mr. Keytes. Pick up your things and come with me this instant!" Mr. Matt marched me out of the classroom and downstairs to the headmaster's office on the ground floor, but his door was locked. "Wait here until Mr. Keytes returns," Mr. Matt said. "I have to return to the classroom."

I am not sure what would have happened if the headmaster had been in his office that afternoon, but my anger and my fear got the better of me. I bolted out of the school and ran almost all the way home. I went straight to my room. Sweat soaked my uniform.

Although it wasn't my day of the week to have a bath, I thought I'd ask Thea. "Please, can I have a quick bath before dinner?" The classroom was very hot today. Mr. Matt wouldn't let us have the windows open, and I sweated a lot."

"Hurry up, and don't use too much hot water."

"Thank you," I said, hurrying upstairs.

I was afraid to go to see the headmaster of my own accord the next day or to go back to my maths class. I reasoned, *Out of sight, out of mind. Mr. Matt won't notice I'm not in class.* I spent my time in the library, telling the librarian I had a free lesson. Because no one came looking for me that day or the next, I continued to go to the library daily. I didn't return to my maths class for the rest of the school year and never told anyone what had occurred that afternoon. I don't remember seeing the girl again or if she reacted to what happened that afternoon, but I never forgot her.

Looking back, I wonder why Thea and Don, my teacher, and the headmaster never communicated with each other about my absence from class. Did they believe I wasn't worth the effort? Or was I invisible to them all? I missed registration (roll call), class time, and exams for at least two months.

I finally took my maths G.C.E in 1990, the same year as my daughter. I needed a passing grade to enter Cambridge University for a teaching certificate programme. I had all my other prerequisites.

1966
Loss

*How do we heal our bruised self-worth and free
ourselves from the words others spoke?*
—Christine M. Kendall

I don't remember being self-conscious about my looks or my hair before coming to England. I didn't have a fringe (bangs) because hair near my eyes had always made me feel ill. As a teenager, still living with Mummy and Daddy in St. Vincent, my hair was always pulled back into a ponytail. I'm not sure why I didn't want to get it cut. Mummy always described my hair as a "rats' tails." It was neither curly nor straight but hung in lank strands of dark, greasy, slightly curled bunches around my face if I didn't pull it up into a tight ponytail. Despite the boys at school who liked to pull girls' hair, it was easy to manage. But I loved it when, after my regular evening shower and before bed, Mummy would roll my hair in rag strips any time I asked her to, which gave my fine, limp hair more body.

She used strips of old cotton sheeting torn into six-inch lengths and about half an inch wide. I would wash my hair and then sit in front of her. She would part and roll up strands of hair in the rags and tie them tight. That's the part that hurt; the short hair got caught in the rags and pulled terribly, but Mummy only smiled and said, "There is no pleasure without pain." I learnt that to have what I wanted, I might have to suffer. I enjoyed my lovely curly hair for a day. It was a tremendous help when I had a test. I twiddled the ringlets around my fingers, stopping my panic from getting out of control when I didn't know the answers.

For the first two years in England, I wore my hair either in a long ponytail or with a wide headband holding the hair off my face. There was another reason I kept my ponytail high and tight: I had a raised scar on the top of my head caused by a birth injury.

During my Fifth year at Hazelwick, someone persuaded me to cut my hair. At first, it looked nice. It was a bob with a fringe, and the sides hung just below my ears; I loved it. For two short months, I raised my head and looked boldly around my teenage world; I felt good. At an extracurricular evening art class, I wore pale lipstick, clear nail varnish, and even a light blue eye shadow—it highlighted the colour of my eyes. I was thrilled that my hair looked fashionable. I would be in my thirties before I realised that I was attractive. Daddy had teased me often, saying, "You get uglier every day." I naively believed he was being honest instead of using emotional avoidance and sarcastic humour.

I was happy when Martin, a boy I liked at school, took an interest in me; I was sixteen. He waited for me after school and we walked partway home together. He also smiled during assembly. I was in seventh heaven. Sadly, it didn't last long.

With six other people in the home, plus a toddler and limited hot water, I found it hard to keep my hair looking nice. I managed to sneak extra bathroom time if I was on my menstruation cycle, but it wasn't enough. My hair didn't behave as I wanted it to. It would curl up in places and down in others. It would get lank and stringy, and Mummy wasn't there to take care of me. Worst, though, I broke out with a nasty red rash along my jawline. I had never had a problem with acne or other skin issues before, and I was distressed. I couldn't put the hair back, so I decided to get it cut shorter, thinking the problems of curls and rashes would be eradicated.

I made an appointment with the local hairdresser, but it was a major disaster. They made a terrible mess of my hair. The finished cut looked like my little sister had attacked it with blunt scissors. It stuck out in short pieces all over my head.

I endured the pain and anguish of sleeping on hair rollers at night, hoping to keep it smooth and in shape. But when I brushed it out in the morning, the cowlicks, which I didn't know I had until then, spun out of control, making me feel like an Abyssinian guinea pig. I was horrified. It was a terrible blow to my sensitive teenage self-esteem. I felt particularly broken when I saw a shocked look on Martin's face as he turned away.

Slowly, my hair grew longer again. I used wax-filled rollers, heated in boiling water, to roll my hair up in the mornings and avoid the nighttime pain. I learnt to back-comb my hair, creating a simpler form of the "beehive" hairstyle.

In my evening art class, I met a young man a few years older than me, who I thought was interesting. We talked effortlessly, which for me was rare and gratifying. His name was Alan. I looked forward to going to those classes every week. Toward the end of the term, Alan told me he was a writer. I was thrilled and replied, "I write poetry."

He asked me to bring some of my poems to class to show him. "I'll bring in some of mine," he said. Alan asked to borrow the book of poetry I'd written. "I'd like to spend some more time reading them without the distraction of our class."

I was excited and agreed instantly. Alan didn't return to class the following week, nor the next, or ever again. I lost everything. I was devastated and cried for days in the privacy of my bedroom, never telling anyone why I was unhappy. All the trust and joy I had begun to build was shattered, and I disappeared into my teenage shell, unable to look boys in the face. I stopped using make-up but continued using the wax rollers and back-combing my hair.

When other girls said, "You'll never have a boyfriend if you don't wear make-up."

I either said nothing or, "I don't care." If a boy only cared about me, all dolled up, I don't want to know him. I threw myself into physical activities like swimming, hiking, and camping.

1967
No Smoke Without Fire

In my last year at Hazelwick Comprehensive School, our athletic teacher had a connection with the South Downs Combined Cadet Forces (CCF). This was a national youth organisation sponsored by the Ministry of Defense and the British Army. Our teacher arranged for four teams from the Upper Fifth and Sixth Form to take part in the "Escape and Evasion" exercises

the CCF organized every year. First, we had to go on
a practise manoeuvre from school in groups of four, on
an overnight hike, from Saturday evening to Sunday
morning. The hike would be approximately ten miles on
minor roads and a few trails going through farms. As an
out-of-doors teenager who went on many long walks,
this sounded like an adventure I did not want to miss. I
asked Graham, a fellow student in my class if he would
be part of my team.

Graham was short and quiet, and I liked him.
We hadn't talked much or spent time together. I was
seventeen and hoped he might ask me out, but he was
also shy. I thought this event might solve the problem.
"Do you have a friend who might like to join us?" I
asked. "I'm going to ask Linda. That will make us a
two-boy, two-girl team." Graham asked his best friend,
William.

At the last minute, Linda backed out, and
Christopher, William's brother, joined us. It would be
the first time I'd met William, as he was in a different
class. I'd seen him around the school many times,
initially not long after starting at Hazelwick. We were
both new at the school and arrived at the main door
late for our morning class. He stammered and shook his
head until the prefect told him, "Just go on, get in, and
go to class." He didn't get detention. I admired what
I thought, at the time, was a perfected act of defiance
to avoid detention. Unable to do anything similar, I'd
stood in front of the prefect with tears of frustration,
knowing I would not be so lucky. How could I explain
that Don, my stepfather, would not be hurried in the

morning, how he kept up continual procrastination after breakfast—I am sure now it was Don's form of control, but maybe he was completely unaware of his behaviour.

For our practise exercise, we started in the village of Maresfield in East Sussex on the evening of March 11th, 1967. We had to make our way to the finish point, a bus stop near the church in Forest Row, where our families or the school coach would collect us. Don said he would take the four of us in his VW Bug and pick us up the next day.

We started walking as one large group of teenagers through the silent wet streets at 10:00 p.m., but it wasn't long before the slower kids fell behind. By midnight, the rain came down rather heavily, and the three boys and I sought shelter under a covered area. We didn't stop for long because we wanted to win the practise run and be chosen for the main event.

We got lost a couple of times near a place called Wych Cross because we discovered a group ahead of us had turned the old-fashioned four-armed intersection road sign around to face a different direction. "We need to pay more attention to our map reading. Let's not get lost again; maybe we can take a shortcut through one of these farms and reach the main road, hopefully ahead of the group that twisted the road sign." I said, studying the map. It was dark and muddy, but we did navigate the numerous stiles through the farms and back to the main road; I believed we were ahead of a few groups.

We walked quite fast most of the time to keep warm, and I ran out of the water I was carrying. I tried catching raindrops in my mouth, but it was a slow and frustrating process. I found a better solution. I lay on my stomach on the deserted street and drank from the puddles. The three boys were mildly disgusted. "What's the matter with you?" I asked. "It's fresh rainwater, isn't it? And I'm thirsty." I was used to improvising and didn't think I would get sick.

I was surprised that Graham, the only guy on my team I knew, didn't try to walk next to me or spend any time talking with me. He always seemed to fall back behind William. I assumed he wasn't interested in me and connected with William instead. He was also quiet, like Graham, but a little less shy. As we sat waiting at the bus stop for Don to arrive at the end of the hike, William put his arm around me, and I fell asleep for a brief period. I felt sorry for Graham. He had a sad face, but he hadn't tried to walk or talk with me except when I spoke to him.

I was still snuggled against William's warm body when Don arrived. The four of us piled in the VW Bug and headed home, dropping Graham off in Crawley and William and Christopher at Three Bridges. "See you in school tomorrow," I said as we waved goodbye.

I have no idea what Don said to Thea about picking us up, but by the time I had taken off my damp clothes, had a bath, and come downstairs, she started giving me the third degree. I was tired, happy, and didn't want to answer any questions. "He's a friend from school, Graham's best friend," I said, followed by, "I am going to sleep for a bit."

I walked away, but as I headed up the stairs, I heard Don say, "There's no smoke without fire." Don was insinuating that our sitting together at the bus stop wasn't as innocent as it appeared.

A couple of days later, Graham, William, and I went on a hike, and William asked me to go to the play *Iolanthe* with him. I was thrilled and didn't care about Don's innuendo. I had a boyfriend now, and I wouldn't be alone anymore. Most importantly, I thought William must like me because I wasn't glamorous during our muddy overnight hike!

All for a Can of Oil

Our team, Graham, Christopher, William, and myself, finished second in the practise manoeuver and qualified to participate in the Escape and Evasion exercise on the South Downs. This time, we would be evading the CCF. I was unaware at the time that I would be the only girl on this twelve-hour, overnight exercise with not only forty seventeen-year-old boys but also burly Army, Navy, and Air Force cadets.

A few weeks later, at the end of April, the teams selected assembled at the Army barracks in Chichester on the South Downs in the early evening. A sergeant major gave us verbal instructions and a secret package, which we were instructed to keep out of the hands of the CCF at all costs. Our team of four, plus two other teams, were loaded into a truck and driven to an outpost some twenty-five to thirty miles from our starting point. The other seven teams went to different outposts.

At the drop-off location, the staff sergeant said, "Avoiding getting caught by the CCF is the aim of the game. Have fun and make it difficult for them." He handed each team a compass, torch (flashlight), and an Ordinance Survey map. "You have a two-hour head start before the cadets begin looking for you. Find your way back to the barracks by morning. Here are your coordinates. We'll have breakfast waiting for you."

Christopher took our covert package. We studied the map, set our compass, and started walking back over the South Downs. The night was dark and moonless, and the stars were beautiful. We carried rain macs and snack rations: chocolate bars, nuts, raisins, and water in our rucksacks. Before the night was over, we would climb over fences, run through people's properties, and fall facedown into ditches to avoid being caught.

William had learnt a little more about map reading since our practise manoeuvre; we didn't plan on getting lost or fooled this time, but we did turn a few signs around to lead others astray! The locals must have hated us for the disruptions caused that night, but we were young. We didn't drive or understand the frustrations of having people tramping through your property, although we always shut the gates behind us.

Around midnight, happily jogging along the road near Pulborough, we heard the sound of a truck on the road some hundred yards behind us. We dived for the ditch, two of us going to one side and two to the other. In total darkness, it was impossible to even make out the other person in the ditch except by smell, little giggles, or whispers.

The truck stopped and ran its searchlights over where we were crouched. We held our breath as the road lit up like daylight. In our dark, grassy chamber, we heard feet jumping from the back of the truck and running up the road. I could see a few house lights on the other side of the street go on. A silhouette of a man's head appeared in an open window, and a voice yelled, "Bloody bastards, sod off out of here."

Little did he know, but that man, whoever he was, saved us that time. The next time, we were not so lucky. There was no ditch alongside the road. The property's edges ran right up to the road, with no pavements (sidewalks). We started running, looking for a place to hide. As the cadets' feet came closer, William and Christopher grabbed me under my arms and dragged me along. But it was not enough. I fell to the ground as one of the cadets tackled me from behind. I screamed.

"Blimey, it's a girl!" The cadet shouted as he leapt to his feet, apologising for knocking me over.

Everyone laughed until the cadet in charge said we were caught and must go with them for interrogation. The three guys had to fend for themselves getting into the truck, but they gave me a boost because the tailgate was almost over my head.

Quietly, I nudged Christopher, "Hand me your rucksack." I placed it on the floor between my feet. I had a plan for hiding the secret package. The cadets drove us a few miles to what looked like an old farm. I faked a stumble as I stood up and kicked the bag under the seat as I got out. I loved detective stories in those days—which inspired the idea.

The four of us were each taken to separate locations on the farm for interrogation. I was taken to a barn and told to wait. "Mind the rats," the cadet laughed as he bolted the door behind him.

I think I was supposed to scream or faint or otherwise be hysterical. Instead, I curled up in a ball and tried to get a little sleep during whatever time was left before the cadets loaded us back on the truck. It helped me from thinking of rats, bats, spiders, or other creatures that might feel I was an intruder in their space.

William revealed later that they made him take his shoes and socks off and walk in what they told him were stinging nettles. He knew that if he walked firmly across the nettles, they wouldn't sting. His friend, Graham, did not fare as well, being more susceptible to mind games. Christopher never explained what "torture" the cadets put him through. Back in the truck, they dropped us off a few miles further along the road from where we were picked up. I stealthily retrieved our secret package from under the seat. We were not caught again. It was a big ego boost when a couple of the cadets congratulated me for not freaking out in the barn.

Although William had been my boyfriend since the practise manoeuvre, on the unpredictable times we had to dive into ditches to avoid contact with the CCF, I ended up nose-to-nose with Christopher. I thought it funny that the person I was least interested in was the person who was always the closest to me. I enjoyed Christopher's light, breezy laugh and how he always helped me back up again when we had the all-clear. It was something I should have paid attention to.

As daylight crept over the hills, a local milkman saw us resting our tired and muddy bodies on a garden wall and offered us a pint of milk each. We gratefully accepted and told him about our night's adventures. We thanked him and watched his empty milk crates rattle as his truck disappeared around the corner before we staggered the last mile to the ACF hut, arriving at 5:45 a.m. We had a lovely breakfast of eggs, sausages, bacon, tomatoes, and mashed potatoes.

Although we were not the first or the last back, we were given a rousing cheer because we were the only team with a girl—and we still had the secret package.

"What is in the package?" I asked.

"Go ahead and open it," the Sergeant Major replied heartily.

Inside the package was a tin can marked "Poison."

"Hi Bill, Graham, Chris, want to see what we have been carrying around all night?" I asked.

"Phew! Glad I didn't know I was lugging that around." Christopher declared with a laugh.

It was a can of nasty, smelly engine oil. Laughter filled the room as Thea, Don, and my four siblings walked in the door. We were ready to go home and sleep. William told me later that he slept for twelve hours!

1965-1969
The Duke of Edinburgh Award

The Duke of Edinburgh's Award (DofE) is a youth programme founded in the United Kingdom by Prince Philip, Duke of Edinburgh, in 1956. The DofE recognises adolescents and young adults aged fourteen to twenty-one for completing a choice of self-improvement exercises based on Kurt Hahn's solutions to his "Six Declines of Modern Youth."* Hahn proposed four solutions to these problems: Fitness Training (to train the discipline and determination of the mind and body); Expeditions (via sea or land to engage in challenging endurance tasks); Projects (involving crafts and manual skills); and Rescue Service (e.g., surf lifesaving, fire fighting, first aid).

John Hunt, who led the earliest successful ascent of Mount Everest in 1953, became the first director of the Duke of Edinburgh Award. The programme was designed to attract boys and, a few years later, girls who were not interested in joining one of the main British youth movements—the Boy Scouts and Girl Guides Associations. Each progressive level demanded more time and commitment from the participants. For the Gold Award, candidates had to complete an additional section, which involved staying and working away from home for at least five days with a group.

According to my diary, I always chose to go above and beyond the requirements for each award. I chose a mix of activities, some I knew I enjoyed and some that were more adventuresome and new to me. Looking back, the work I did then helped me test my limits, enhance my skills, help the community, and grow in confidence.

As previously mentioned, I did my Bronze Expedition by completing an overnight march with the

* Kurt Hahn. (2023, June 11). Wikipedia. https://en.wikipedia.org/wiki/Kurt_ Hahn#Philosophy.

Tulse Hill Army Cadets, travelling from London to Winterdown. For my interests, I continued to pursue my swimming certifications. I completed my Bronze, Silver, and Gold Proficiencies in personal survival. The Design for Living—a girls-only section—covered health, hygiene, and good manners. Learning how to make an invisible patch, plus hand and machine darns. I also created a booklet of what to wear to work and the costs of the complete ensemble. For my service to the community, I took a basic first-aid course with the Girl Guides.

For the Silver level, I took a badminton class for one of my interests and another in upholstery for the Design for Living. I extended my service section from basic first aid to child welfare with the St. John's Ambulance. I completed a two-day expedition over the South Downs with three other girls. We carried two tents and the equipment and food we would need for two days and one overnight. One girl, a bubbly scatterbrain called Barbara, took hair curlers and a dryer (which she couldn't use, of course)—there are no electricity sockets in nature!

I was between seventeen and eighteen when I started working on my DofE Gold Award. I completed a portion of this final award before I finished school and continued after I left, went to work, and trained as a cadet. Don and Thea were the official supervisors of our expedition, but the rest I organized out of personal interest and desire.

My Gold Expedition was one of the best and most exhausting expeditions I did in my first five years in England. It made me feel strong and invincible, especially as this expedition made history: five teenagers—three girls and two boys—were the first team to do a mixed expedition. Four of us—Geoff, Irene, Anne, and I—lived in Crawley, Sussex. Guy, the fifth person, lived in London. Together with Don, Thea, and the family, we left Crawley and drove to the village of Edale, Derbyshire, a wild part of the north of England in the 1960s. It was pouring rain when we arrived at our base camp.

We pitched our two tents and cooked supper on a single Campingaz stove, alternating and stacking the pans to keep the meal hot. We had mixed grill and potatoes that first night. For dessert, mandarin flan cake and cream. We knew how to eat in style when camping in those days. We were in bed and asleep by 9:00 p.m. In the morning, we three girls cooked breakfast of porridge and scrambled eggs and were ready to start our first orientation by 7:00 a.m. It was another wet day. By the time we finished our first hike, we were soaked to our underclothes. The tents, left up while we were gone, were floating in water. Our extra clothes and food were saturated. The loo (bathroom) looked like a laundry with clothes hanging everywhere.

The boys and I cooked supper that night, and the vicar of the local church offered to dry out our sleeping bags and clothes while we went off to join Thea and Don at the Nag's Head pub for a drink. Accompanied by an adult, we could have a shandy—a combination of lager and lemonade or a glass of wine.

We restocked our food store and re-packed our

rucksacks. We divided the tents, food, and equipment equally among the five of us ready for our fifty-mile hike, as the crow flies, through the bleak wilderness of the Peak District. We would be on our own for the duration of the expedition.

At 8:00 a.m. on Wednesday 30th October 1968, we marked our first checkpoint by leaving a pennant (flag) on Don's car and set off—our packs weighed about thirty pounds each.

Progress was slow as we climbed 829 feet up Mam Tor, which means Mother Hill, so named because of ancient landslides, which created a multitude of mini hills beneath the eastern slope. We stopped at the top for a rest and to eat sweets. We continued along Rushup Edge, then a hard slog through the boggy peat towards Brown Knoll. Irene took a wrong step and sank to her knees in the peat bog. It took three of us to pull her out.

We all took turns mapping our route. We had to use our compasses because of the heavy mist blotting the valley below. After deciding which path to take, we made our way along Kinder Reservoir, down William Clough, a deep sided valley, up the steep shale snake path feeling like mountain goats, and down to our first campsite opposite the Snake Inn. We had walked twelve and a half miles in nine hours and forty-five minutes. We put up our tents and made supper: spaghetti bolognese and runner beans, followed by a large slice of fruit cake and coffee. Delicious! We were in our sleeping bags by 9:00 p.m. The next day would be our longest: sixteen miles in ten hours.

We had our usual hearty breakfast, broke camp,

and were on our way by 8:00 a.m. It rained most of the day, but we managed a great lunch of liver sausage in bread rolls, cheese, fruit cake, coffee, and Cadbury's fruit and nut chocolate. I started the day with dry socks, but within two hours of walking, lines of white foam oozed through my thick wool socks into the creases of my leather boots.

The gates at Blackshaw Farm were wired shut, leaving only a narrow opening for hikers, but our packs were too large to fit through. The rest of the team was tall enough to hoist their packs onto their shoulders and squeeze through. I was shorter, unable to raise my arms high enough to get through without help.

When we crossed Salters Brook, the usually slow-moving stream was a rushing river. By the end of the day, we were hungry and exhausted. After eating, we squeezed the water out of our clothes and placed them in a canvas bag under our sleeping bags. Our body heat would dry the clothes overnight. We fell into our sleeping bags, and despite the lumpy ground, we went to sleep quickly.

On our last day, I woke to feel our tent floating. The wind whipped the flysheet, and the rain beat down, playing tom-tom music on the mess tins outside the tents. Nothing was dry, and the temperature was zero degrees centigrade. While the boys took down the tents, we three girls struggled to get dressed in the cramped farmer's barn. We used up all the remaining porridge, stirring the extra sugar lumps into it. The farmer gave us six fresh eggs, which we scrambled along with our five. We threw away the bread because it was soggy. After breakfast, we cleaned the dishes, packed up, and headed out despite the torrential downpour.

The beautiful Ladybower Reservoir overflowed its bank that year, causing widespread flooding. We finished the last seven miles in an hour and a half, hiking on the A57 and singing at the top of our voices. Back at base camp, we changed into the dry clothes we'd left behind. Threw all the wet stuff into the back of Don's caravan and headed home. I went straight to bed and slept for twelve hours without waking up.

We had a lot of fun, plus a few weird experiences: Geoff calling out in his sleep, asking me where we were, and me answering him. Anne and I warming our hands in Guy's armpits, and the time we took down and packed up the tents following a wet night in a cow field. We climbed 6,620 feet and walked forty-eight miles in thirty-one hours while carrying our food and camping equipment on our backs in the rain!

Two of my siblings, Tina, age fourteen, and Derek, age fifteen, also took part in an expedition for their Bronze Award. They hiked sixteen miles and climbed 760 feet in two days, camping overnight in tents. Tina made history by completing a much harder expedition than usually undertaken by girls. Tina told the newspaper, "I'm wet through, frozen, but all right!"

In addition to the expedition, I wrote a thirty-page booklet on the geology of the Peak District and a short chapter on prehistoric man in the area before the arrival of the Romans, which marks the division between early humans and recorded history.

As part of my Gold, I did a historical survey of my

hometown, Crawley and created a portfolio on how to self-build or buy a house. I covered all the how-tos:—the surveyors, the solicitors, the costs, room plans, materials, and furnishings. I would use much of what I collected later in life. Plus, a two-year cadet training to become a Girl Guide leader. I also completed a practical course on everyday nursing: how to care for individuals from infants to elderly. My final section to complete my Gold DofE was a residential course in Burwash, East Sussex.

I completed my Duke of Edinburgh Award in May 1969. I received the invitation for the awards presentation at Buckingham Palace in July of the same year while living in lodging in Salford. Dick Fuller, one of the youth leaders from Crawley, accompanied me as I was no longer living with Thea or Don.

The awards ceremony was held in Buckingham Palace Gardens. Hundreds of other young adults received their awards that day. I didn't meet or see the Queen, but Prince Philip did speak to me directly and asked if I had enjoyed the scheme. Of course, I replied that I had.

1968
Burwash Place
A Residential Course for the Education of Girls

I chose to do a seven-day residential course in Burwash Place in Sussex. It was a beautiful old building with an expansive garden. I was one of twenty-six girls from all over the country who took the course. The fees for the week were just over £7, which included lodging, food, and instruction.

I remember one girl in particular. She had long fingernails, especially the little fingernail on her right hand. It was over two inches long and curled under. I was fascinated by her because she was a typist and had never cut her nails since she'd stopped biting them. She'd also hitch-hiked from her home in northern England. It was something I was afraid to do.

An eccentric older lady collected five or six of us from the Etchingham Railway Station in her Morris Minor. We were squeezed in like sardines, which was fortunate because she drove fast and erratically. Each time she pointed out a place of interest, the steering wheel followed her finger. We almost left the road and went into a ditch more than once. She seemed to be enjoying the shrieks and screams of the girls as we lurched along the narrow road.

Three of us, Judith, Anne, and I, spent two days and a night at Park Wood, a dairy, beef cattle, and hop farm. The farmhouse was in an idyllic site—a saddle between the hills with a view of the famous Puck Hill around which Rudyard Kipling's *Puck of Pook's Hill,* a series of short children's stories set in different periods of English history, was written and published in 1906.

Our first job at the farm was to sort out the perfect hop-hooks from the broken and badly twisted ones. Farmer Walphem was very pleased with our 150 good ones. Our next job was a lot heavier. We filled hessian (burlap) bags with rocks from the unploughed field above the farmhouse and carried them down the hill to the gate. It was to be a hay field in the summer. Removing the stones prevented damage to the harvester. We were exhausted when we finished. Later, we helped the farmer's son, Clive, put in a barbed-wire fence to protect the site of his future home from the cows.

We all had the opportunity to drive the tractor; Judith and Anne did well. I liked to think they had both driven before because when it was my turn, I didn't apply the clutch and brake properly, stalled, and shot Anne and Judith off the back end of the tractor.

We spent that night in the hay barn. The following morning, there was ice on the puddles. I was the only one who stayed warm because I knew how to prevent cold air pockets. Although quite prickly, I burrowed into the straw to keep warm.

The next day, Clive showed us around the farm. We fed the chickens and took turns riding the horse. I was a bit leery after my childhood experience of riding a donkey that had thrown me into a pond. We watched the farmer milk forty cows. Suckers (teat cups) were attached to four cows at a time. The milk was pumped from the cow into a large glass cylinder. From there, it went into a metal cooler with cold water running through it and then into churns. This was the last we saw of the milk before it went to an outside dairy to be bottled for market.

A couple of days later, much to my embarrassment, I received a letter from Clive during breakfast, simply addressed: TO JANE MOLLER OF CRAWLEY. In it, he wrote, "I will never forget the day I first saw you...

." He professed his undying love and wanted to take me out on his motorbike—I had helped Clive fix his tyre the day before and was surprised by its pink hubcaps. The thought of being on the bike with him scared me. I didn't reply or go back to the farm, and when Clive showed up in Crawley a week later looking for me, I panicked and stayed indoors for a few days.

We went on an educational trip to Bateman House, the home of Rudyard Kipling. This Jacobean house, built in 1634, is set in the beautiful landscape of the Sussex Weald. Twelve acres of gardens surround the house, which features a river, a wildflower meadow, a watermill, an orchard, a lily pond, and a formal rose garden. I was in awe of the incredible beauty of Kipling's home. He wrote, "It makes me feel like an English country gentleman." The interior included his study and the library where he penned the wonderful poem "IF"—*If you can keep your head when all about you are losing theirs* … The dining room had embossed leather wall hangings that, when polished, shone like gold. Kipling was proud of these walls and remarked, "It is lovelier than our wildest dreams and will need immense care."

We listened to a lecture on the local history before we went to a sheep farm in Rye, an ancient coastal town built at the confluence of three rivers: the Rother, the Tillingham, and the Brede. Rye was part of the Saxon Manor of Rameslie, given to the Benedictine Abbey of Fécamp in Normandy by King Æthelred. Rye was originally located on a long embayment of the English

Channel called the Rye Camber, which provided safe anchorage and harbour.

In Roman times, the town was an important port for the Wealden iron industry. Violent storms in the 13th century cut Rye off from the sea. Today, it is situated at least two miles inland. The high taxes on material goods encouraged smuggling, and the famous Mermaid Inn in Rye is full of smuggler stories of the notorious Hawkhurst Gang.

We also learnt that when the River Rother's flow changed in 1287 from its easterly course, the area became known as the Romney Marsh, which extended over 5,000 acres. In the past, two-thirds were ploughed, and a third grassed. It was kept short because it was unfit for sheep grazing once seeded. Romney sheep were exported globally—they were considered the most successful breeds. The main characteristic was their ability to feed in wet situations, making them resistant to foot rot and internal parasites.

In the 18th and 19th centuries, men known as "lookers" were hired to care for large flocks of sheep on the Romney Marsh. Together with their dogs, they lived in huts about ten feet square. These huts had a tiled roof, a small window, and a chimney for a fireplace. These temporary dwellings were necessary at lambing time. In 1870, 356 lookers' huts were recorded—few are left today.

After the lecture, twelve of the group headed to Mr. Catt's sheep farm for the final class of the week. He had 450 ewes. Mr. Catt rented two rams to "work his flock." Each ram could inseminate a hundred ewes in a day. "They arrive on November 5th* and go to work with a bang," he said with a cocky smile. Lambing started in early spring. As the lambs were born, a clip was put into each ear, one with the Romney Marsh registration and the other with the year and order of birth. Twins were daubed with paint on their heads for easy recognition. Small rubber rings were placed on the lamb's tail, close to the buttocks, restricting the blood flow—they dropped off in about three weeks. The sheep are shorn in July and August. Ewes yield nine and a quarter pounds of wool, and lambs, a pound and a half. Once the sheep are shorn, they are dipped in a disinfectant which stops the flies.

On our last full day at Burwash Place, the whole group went to Harrison Rocks, a popular climbing area south of the village of Groombridge. Harrison Rocks are a series of sandstone crags and a great example of a periglacial landform. I had mixed feelings before we left because I'd never been rock climbing. Our guide taught us the best way to stand when belaying (holding the rope while another person climbed), giving the climber slack if the line was too tight, and coiling it so it wouldn't kink. At the rocks, we were divided into two groups, and I started on a B1, a second-grade climb. The hardest is a B6. By the end of the day, I managed a B2 chimney climb. It was a lot of fun—great teamwork and pleasant exercise. I remember it with fondness.

---

* November 5th is Guy Fawkes Day. It celebrates the failed 17th-century attempt to blow up Parliament and assassinate King James I with fireworks.

2010
Enemy in the House

Memory often surprises me. Sometimes, the tiniest thing will trigger a memory from a long time ago.

My granddaughter and I were going to church, but she was taking a long time to get ready. "If you are not dressed in one minute flat," I called through the door, "we'll be late." Then she told me we had to make a stop at the store.

"Now?" I exclaimed, "Can't we go after?"

"No, I just started my period," she answered.

"O.K, sorry. Let's hurry, then we'll only be a little late."

My granddaughter obliged, and off we drove. She hurried into the store and returned a few minutes later with a small packet of tampons.

I had a sudden flashback: I was seventeen, just two-and-a-half years older than my granddaughter.

—

It was 1967. I had been in England with my birth mother, Thea, her common-law husband, Don, and my four half-siblings for three years. I was beginning to feel that I might fit at last. I even had a boyfriend.

Discussing women's issues was taboo in our home. The subject was rarely discussed and only behind closed doors, but I was desperate. I had a swimming competition, and my monthly bleeding had just started. The sanitary towels I usually wore couldn't be worn under a swimsuit for obvious reasons. The thought of explaining to my swimming coach why I would be unable to compete sent me into a panic. My sister was too young, and I wouldn't talk to my brother about this. His interest in my feminine body terrified me.

Eventually, I got enough courage to go to Thea and ask her, "What can I do?"

She gave me a single tampon and the empty packet. "This will explain how to insert the tampon," she said. "The kids won't disturb you. They are in the living room doing their homework." She told me to go practise in the bathroom.

I chose to use the upstairs bathroom. It was the closest to my bedroom, which was unfortunate because Don came home and refused to use the downstairs loo. His shouts and my tears brought Thea to the scene. She eventually had to explain to Don why I could not leave the bathroom in a hurry. It was at this point that my predicament became a nightmare. As I tried to slip unnoticed into my bedroom, Don said, "You stay in your room while I talk to your mother."

I could hear Don doing most of the talking. I heard words like, "She can't be a virgin. She's your daughter. She's a whore." He used other words associated with "loose women." There was silence for a while. Then, I heard Don and Thea leave their room and go downstairs. I was left alone in my room, not daring to leave in case Don might lose his temper.

He came back upstairs and walked into my bedroom without knocking. "So, you're a woman now. You'll stay in your room without supper. I don't want you downstairs contaminating the others."

Don upset the whole household and made my world public hell. In the morning, before I left for school, Thea, who had not intervened to help me the previous day, handed me a small case containing two tampons. Don had already left for work. "That will get you through the day," she said.

I did compete in the swimming competition and won a few awards, which I hid when I reached home. I found a hiding spot under a loose board in my clothes closet. For the next couple of years, while I was still at home, this is where I kept my tampons and other secret things.

When I went out on a Saturday night with my boyfriend, my curfew was 11:00 p.m. We usually went to the Saturday movie in Redhill, a short train ride away, and we could make it back in time, but the weekend the clocks went forward, we made an error. Thea and Don always put the clocks back early, so according to them, I was an hour late when I walked in that night. They were waiting for me. They both refused to listen that it wasn't midnight yet. There was an ugly scene with a lot of shouting. I went to bed in disgrace and tears.

The following day, when I ran upstairs to my room, Don called through his bedroom door, "Can you come here a minute? I need to show you something." He was getting ready to go out for the evening.

He sat on the bed, wearing only his shirt, "Come here. Your mother and I have decided I should talk to you about boys."

I stood away from him, saying nothing.

"We want you to know what to expect when you are with your boyfriend."

I did not move.

"Give me your hand."

I backed up against the wall, putting my hands behind my back.

"It is all right. You know your mother's only downstairs," he said as he leaned forward, grabbed one of my hands, and pulled me towards him, placing my hand on his erect penis.

It was wet and revolting. I recoiled in horror and pulled my hand away as I backed up against the bedroom door, preparing to flee or scream. Before I could do either, he said, "When you feel William's body bulging against you, you'll know what you have done. It will be your fault when he can't stop."

My life in the household changed from that day onwards. I never talked about the incident. What could I say? Don told me he and Thea had discussed the subject of boys. If Don was the only one at home, I left. Many a time, I went without a meal, going for long walks until it was dark and someone else was at home.

Years later, I found out that what he could not do with me, he, unfortunately, did with my siblings. When there's an enemy in the house, the guilt lasts a lifetime and affects us all differently.

1969
Without Shoes

It was a bitterly cold night in February. My curtains were tightly closed. I had a hot water bottle at my feet and behind my back. I kept my blankets wrapped tightly around my body while I wrote to Mummy and Daddy. I told them about my plans to visit at Christmas that year and the lovely blue iris flowers William had given me for Valentine's Day. We'd been going steady for almost two years. I hadn't told Thea and Don about my plans to go home to see Mummy and Daddy; when I did a couple of weeks later, I was surprised by Don's apparent displeasure and Thea's silence. During the next few weeks, I felt even the air in the house was tense!

On March 29th, I went to William's parents' home to watch the "Eurovision Song Contest." I had a wonderful evening with my boyfriend and his family. It was the first time in history that the voting resulted in four countries tied for first place. I don't remember the other three countries, but the United Kingdom won with the song "Boom Bang-a-Bang" by Lulu, a Scottish singer.

I walked home alone in the falling snow with a smile of joy and love in my heart. Everyone at home was already asleep as I tiptoed up the stairs and slipped into bed, happy and content.

In the morning, sunshine sparkled over a thick layer of snow. I expected to hear my siblings playing outside but I heard nothing, not even a sound from their rooms. *Why was it so quiet?* I felt nervous. *What happened last night?* I got up, slipped into the bathroom, and checked the bedrooms. It looked like the children were still under the covers. Thea was downstairs in the living room.

"Good morning, I'm just going to get myself something to eat. It looks lovely outside," I said. I had only gone a few steps before Thea lashed out at me.

"Where the hell were you all night?"

"Upstairs, asleep, where else would I be?"

I didn't understand why Thea thought I had stayed out all night. Did she forget where I had gone for the evening, or did I forget to do something I was supposed to do? Her implied accusation made me angry. I should have remained silent and let her words wash over me, but I didn't. "Why are you shouting at me? I wasn't late. It's you who went to bed early. You always ruin it when I have a wonderful evening."

Thea looked up, a startled look on her face; it looked like she hated me or someone. Her eyes were red and wild. We were now standing in the hallway. I tried to run up the stairs to my room, but she grabbed me by the arm and opened the front door. "Out," she screamed, "just get out!"

I had no time to change into my shoes or grab my coat. I knocked on the door. "I need my shoes and coat, please."

"Here," she said, opening the door and flinging my coat onto the snow.

I picked it up. "Thank you, I'll be at William's,"

I said and left. I didn't want to ask again about my shoes. I walked the two miles to his parents' house, still wearing my slippers. My feet were wet and freezing when I reached their house. William's mother, June, quickly made me a hot cup of tea. She added a lot of sugar, which was awful, but I didn't mention it.

William must have picked up some clothes the next day for me, and I stayed at his home for a week and then with friends Brian and Renee. They had two boys, approximately four and six years younger than me. Their father was the older brother of my best friend, Linda.

For most of April that year, I was in perpetual motion, moving back and forth between William's family and my friends. Brian offered me a permanent place in their home, but I didn't think my presence in the household was tenable. I was beginning to fall in love with Brian because he was a kind and gentle man. I remember being surprised that he always made the tea and cooked the meals. I wasn't a homewrecker, and I loved William. I found a room to let in Salfords near my work and moved out.

My only steadfast emotional support for the rest of 1969 was William. I moved into a lovely upstairs room in the home of a workmate's grandparents, Within a few days, I realised that I had done what Mummy called "Jumping from the frying pan into the fire." I don't remember the couple's names, but I'll call them Arthur and Rose. I assumed that they were probably in their late sixties. Arthur's hair was already gray, but Rose's looked dyed bronze-brown. I thought she wore a lot of make-up, but so did her granddaughter, Cindy.

I never forgot our daily meals. How could I? Rose cooked the same food without variation each day of every week and put it on to cook at the same time in the afternoon. The minced beef in gravy on Tuesdays was the best, but cabbage cooked for four hours was not. The day after I moved in, Rose told me, "At weekends, you can come back to sleep, but I don't want you here during the day." Rose made me feel irrelevant.

William would pick me up on Saturday mornings in his old green Hillman Imp. We'd hang out during the day and go to the pictures in the evening. Afterwards he'd drop me back at the house around 11:30 p.m. Rose was always waiting for me when I came in, accusing me of "carrying on" outside her bedroom window. "Cindy would never sit outside in a car with her boyfriend." I felt she was implying I was a bad person.

Hah, I thought. *Little does she know what Cindy and her boyfriend get up to!* But I wasn't about to tell on a workmate.

Arthur was a sweetheart. I loved listening to him tell stories about his life. As a young man, he was a contractor; he built their house, which cost him £400. He also talked about making cider from the apples in his garden. But Rose didn't like us talking together, "It's not proper for a girl to take an interest in what a man does," she said. I ignored Rose's comments and innuendos until some weeks later when an assumption on her part made me furious.

I had an interview with a doctor at Redhill Hospital to discuss the removal of the pyramid of skin on the top of my skull caused by the doctor's use of the amnihook to hasten my birth. Although I had never thought much about the scar, when Anne, my sister/ aunt, suggested that I have it removed, and William' commented, "It will be nicer to run my hands through your hair if it is removed." I was convinced.

Rose decided I had gone for an abortion when I didn't tell her I was taking a day off work. She added two and two and came up with six. I was startled at first, then angry at being misjudged. "You have a nasty mind," I shouted at her. "It's none of your business why I took a day off or what I did with my time. It is your conduct that makes you accuse me. Maybe you should ask your granddaughter what she did with her boyfriend on her mother's kitchen table. It's not something I would do." I paused for breath, "I think you owe me an apology."

Rose walked away without saying another word. She turned off the television. It was a Wednesday night, and the show we usually watched together—"It Takes a Thief with Robert Wagner, was on. I did not go upstairs but sat quietly in the living room until 9:00 p.m. when the film would have finished.

I left that house at the end of the week to stay with Anne in Forest Row. I would care for Jeanne-Marie while Anne worked at the local hospital.

1969
End of an Era

L iving with Anne was like being with a rum-
bling volcano, but I loved her almost as much
as Mummy and Daddy. As a child, I'd enjoyed being
with her and her children, Bruce and Jeanne-Marie, in
Trinidad. Anne was spontaneous and fun. Yet, she was
unpredictable; she could lash out at something one day
that had been acceptable the previous day. I believed
Anne was frustrated and lonely—Jerry, her husband,
was never around. He spent at least six months abroad
each year and never spent time with his children when
they were small.

It was an easy decision to move in with Anne
because William rented a tiny flat nearby and worked
at the hospital. I could also save all my wages. Anne
worked evenings and weekends as a nurse in the burns
unit at East Grinstead Hospital.* I missed Bruce, but he
was away at boarding school or camp for almost all the
months I stayed with Anne.

Jeanne-Marie, the beautiful baby I had known in
St. Vincent, was now nine years old. The years of family
isolation, living in Tortola, the British Virgin Islands,
since her reaction as a baby to the Salk vaccine, had
taken its toll on her body—encephalitis had left her
semi-paralysed and with grand mal seisures.

She was no longer the wild animal she had

---

*It became a world-famous hospital for the pioneering treatment of Royal Air Force
and allied aircrew who were burned or crushed and required reconstructive plastic
surgery.

seemed when Anne and the children had first arrived in England in late 1965. Back then, I had been terrified of Jeanne-Marie—she bit and scratched like a feral cat caught in a trap while Bruce fought her off.

I felt sorry for Bruce because Anne was so caught up in the care of her daughter he was often neglected. Unless Jeanne-Marie went into an institution for the mentally disabled, which Anne wasn't prepared to do, there was little respite for her. The medication for Jeanne-Marie's grand mal seisures kept her behaviour in check, but she had little schooling. It would be a few more years before she could spell and read simple words.

Jeanne-Marie was a delight to take care of most of the time. She loved to sing, go for walks, and cuddle up between William and me on the couch. We didn't have a television, so I read many children's books to her. But Jeanne-Marie was very spoilt and used to getting her way most of the time; Anne was afraid of her having seisures. One day, while in the home alone with Jeanne-Marie, I saw her deliberately pitch herself down the last few stairs and into the hall radiator because she hadn't got what she wanted. I was angry and scared. I dragged her to her feet, shouting at her, "You did that on purpose. Don't ever do that to me or your Mum again." Later, I read one of Aesop's fables to her: "The Little Boy Who Cried Wolf." At the end of the story, I said. "Don't ever try to trick me again." She never did, and I didn't tell Anne.

My surgery was scheduled for November at Redhill Hospital. When I went in, I thought the hospital smelt unpleasant, and the paint was old and chipped. I remember lying on a table with bright lights overhead and a man in a white coat saying, "Start counting backwards," as he placed a mask over my face. I woke up in a ward with about six other surgical patients and William sitting on a chair beside my bed. It was nearly supper time, and the nurse asked if I wanted something to eat. The onion soup offered smelt and tasted delicious. I finished the soup but promptly brought it all up. It was messy, but I still felt good. William and I laughed about it before he went to find a nurse to clean up the bed.

Once the nurse changed the sheets, visiting hours were almost over. As William started to say goodbye, my neck arched, my eyes rolled backwards, and my hands clenched. I was petrified. Was my brain going to be permanently damaged? Was I going to be like Jeanne-Marie?

I began to cry, and William called the nurse. She told William to leave immediately and whipped the privacy curtains around me. "Be quiet. You are disturbing the other patients," she said, sticking a needle into my arm. When I woke up, it was dark, and an older nurse was on duty. She was motherly with a lovely big smile. She put an arm around me and gently steered me to the toilet. She told me I would be OK, and that a lady named Anne Lomer had called to see how I was.

"That's my sister," I said.

"She'll be coming in the morning to take you home. It's too late now."

I remember thinking William must be scared out of his mind. Later, he told me he talked to Anne

and Thea before he went home that evening. He said
they got into a terrible argument, accusing each other
of neglect. Neither of them ever told me about the
altercation. The episode turned out to be the after-
effects of the anesthetic. If only the doctor had said
that the anesthesia, probably halothane (discovered in
the 1960s) might have a strange effect on my body as it
wore off.

Jane's mother, Thea and baby
Sophie, August,1964.

Jane, school photo, age 16.

Jane on *Wairakei II* beneath Westminster
Bridge.

Jane, just enrolled as a Girl
Guide 1964.

Leaving for Meschede. Barbara, Jane and Theresa.

Jane, age 15 with Dorothea, age 13.

Jane and her Girl Guide Company, 1968.

Gold Expedition in the Peak District.
From left to right: Guy, Geoff, Irene
Anne, and Jane in front.

Girl Guide leader's training
camp.

Jane's Girl Guide awards
and badges.

Halfway through a Duke of Edinburgh Award Scheme expedition in the Peak District, Geoffrey Snell (left), Jane Moller, Anne Reeves, Guy Wilson and Irene Church have slogged 35 miles through mist and rain.

GIRLS MAKE HISTORY IN PEAK DISTRICT 'SLOG'

Hikers making headlines.

The shoes tell the story. A slog, indeed.

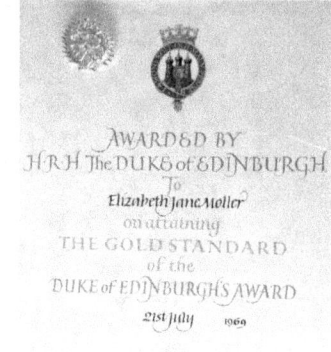

AWARDED BY
H·R·H The DUKE of EDINBURGH
To
Elizabeth Jane Moller
on attaining
THE GOLD STANDARD
of the
DUKE of EDINBURGH'S AWARD
21st July 1969

Jane and the Duke of Edinburgh Gold award with the pin
in the left hand corner.

Reception for the presentation
of Gold Standard Awards
by HRH The Duke of Edinburgh

Admit bearer to
Buckingham Palace
on Monday 21st July, 1969

Bureau through the Royal Mews Entrance from 2 p.m.
Guests are asked to be in position by 2.50 p.m.
CAMERAS NOT ALLOWED

This card must be presented for admittance to the Palace

The Equerry-in-Waiting to The Duke of Edinburgh
is desired by His Royal Highness to invite

Elizabeth Moller

to attend the presentation of Awards
to young people who have reached the Gold Standard
in His Royal Highness's Award Scheme

in the Garden of Buckingham Palace
at 3 p.m. on Monday 21st July 1969

Dress: Lounge Suit or Uniform, Afternoon Dress

Jane's invitation to the palace to receive her Gold Award
from Prince Philip. She was 19.

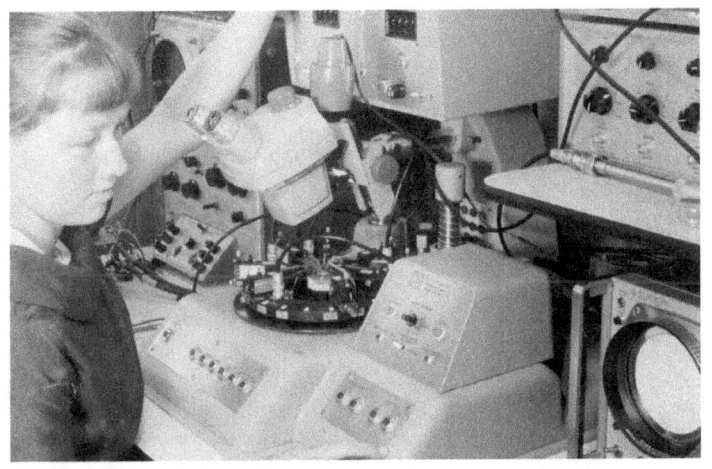

Jane testing circuit breakers at her job at the Philip's Company. This photo went to the Netherlands for an exposition in the 1970s.

1969–1970

Return
to my Island
Home

Going Home

A few weeks later, I booked a direct flight to Barbados on a West Indian charter flight for December 13th. I bought a one-way flight for £100, as I didn't plan on returning in three weeks. The journey was awful. The plane was packed with people, and the space between the seats was minimal. I was cramped and uncomfortable, and my head felt like it would explode with the pressure of the take-off.

When I touched down in Barbados, my brother/uncle, Douglas, his wife, Nadine, and their three boys were there to meet me. I spent a few days with them before flying to St. Vincent. I loved my time with Douglas and his family because they made such a fuss over me. On the day of my arrival, the boys took me to a party in the evening, but I had trouble staying awake since I hadn't slept for thirty-six hours. Years later, I dreamed that my birth father was at that party and that I was introduced to him. However, I had no way of knowing if that was true as I didn't learn his name until I was in my forties.

There were countless things I wanted to see and do now that I was back in the islands—seeing Douglas and his family after so long, exploring Bridgetown, surfing at the beach, and attending parties at night. It was a teenage world filled with joy and fun, and I cherished the experience.

The fireflies were beautiful; hundreds flitted in and out of the trees around Doug and Nadine's home at night. There were so many they blotted out the stars in the early evening. I felt a huge sigh of contentment fill my body that night when I saw the Southern Cross in the sky.

A few days later, I walked across the tarmac from the small Leeward Island Air Transport (LIAT) aircraft on the Arnos Vale runway. Daddy met me outside the terminal.

"Hi, Janie."

"Hi, Daddy," I noticed his eyes immediately. They still looked the same—bright blue, otherwise a little older and redder in the face. He smelt the same—of sunshine, cigarettes, and Limacol Aftershave. Beneath Daddy's shorts, I noticed the bandages were higher up on his legs. The fungal patches he had when I left home must have spread.

"Why didn't Mummy come?"

"She's getting our dinner."

There was a moment of awkward silence, then we hugged, got into his car, and drove away. I don't recall talking much during our journey out of town. It seemed to take a long time as it was already dark when we got to their home in Cumberland—I had never seen this place. I was finally home, but it felt different and strange.

Cumberland

The house in the hills of Cumberland was older, bigger, and more remote than when I lived in St. Vincent nearly six years ago. The nearest English neighbours lived miles away on a twisty drive, up and down hills and across a river on the way into Kingstown.

When I first saw Mummy, her eyes startled me. They seemed so tiny, hidden in folds of flesh. Their brilliant blue had faded to almost gray. She had lost weight, and the skin of her arms hung loose, like curtains, off her bones. Her hair was thin and grayer. It was so different from the vision I had held in my heart for five years while in England, but she still smelt of eau de cologne when I hugged her.

For the days before Christmas, our highlight of the week was when Daddy drove Mummy and me into town on Tuesdays and Thursdays. Breakfast was early and cheerful. On the drive into town, Mummy and I sang old country-style songs or "Hey Jude," her favourite, from the Beatles, and "Here Comes the Sun." Daddy's only comment was usually, "Stop yer caterwauling." Yet, his eyes twinkled, his round face bright and happy. I also liked the number one song that month, "Someday We'll Be Together" by Diana Ross and the Supremes. It made me think of William, back in England.

During that first week, Daddy didn't stop to buy the Mount Gay Rum he drank before I left the island—he seemed excited to have me home. On our first trip into town, Daddy stopped at the cigarette factory on the way to the Aquatic Club. He picked up his cigarettes, and we talked with some of the ladies I knew before I left. Afterwards, I went for a swim, and then we headed back into town to collect a few groceries and pick up paintbrushes and scrapers. Daddy suggested that I could make the bathroom look much better than it did. "It will keep you out of mischief," he'd said with a smile.

Before I started, dirt laid siege to the bathroom. It clotted every crevice and clung to the windowpanes. I spent the next week, between reading and taking short walks into the hills, scraping dirt and paint, and prepping the windows and walls in the bathroom, which were moldy and flaky from the moisture. We had a lovely, brightly coloured bathroom with white windowsills, just in time for Christmas.

It was lovely to wake up on Christmas Day to warm sunshine. I'd put up a tree and a few special ornaments the night before. We had our usual meal from so many years ago: chicken, fresh vegetables, and Mummy's delicious Christmas pudding— she had made it especially because I was home. I brought them a record of Vivaldi's *Four Seasons* from England, which they both loved. Boxing Day was quiet. Mummy and Daddy were up early as usual. We had a lovely breakfast of paw-paw (papaya), Nescafé, and crepes with lime juice and Demerara sugar—a little piece of heaven. Afterwards, I went for a walk until it started raining.

I came in, took a shower, and joined Mummy in reading for the rest of the day. Daddy tinkered with the car and read the newspaper. Mummy's favourite author at the time was Lucy Walker, an Australian

writer born Dorothy Lucie McClemans. She wrote
19th-century romance stories. Mummy loved them for
their "Outback" setting. She and Daddy had spent many
years in the Australian Outback with their Children,
Lorna, Anne, Douglas, and my mother, Althea. I could
read two Lucy Walker books in a day.

On Tuesday, December 30th, we went into town to
stay in a home called the White House; Mummy was
the caretaker while the owners were in Europe. I went
to an awesome dance on Old Year's Night (New Year's
Eve). I wore a full-length, spaghetti-strap gold lamé
dress that Mummy helped me cut out and sew in a day.
I had an incredible time dancing with many friends. It
was nice to see the young people I knew five years ago,
especially Noel, the brother of my friend Gloria from
Calliaqua. I had always liked him. He was part of the
band playing that night. Then there was Andrew, the
older brother of a friend from my old convent school
days. I enjoyed dancing with him that evening. He was
a good dancer with a firm hold guiding me around the
floor. I didn't get home until 5:00 a.m.

I slept late and then spent the afternoon with
friends, not returning until after 10:00 p.m. I was
happy and surprised that neither Mummy nor Daddy
commented on my lateness—nothing like Thea
and Don. We returned the next day to Cumberland
to find we had no electricity. I was shocked, but
apparently, outages happened often since they moved
into the house. I spent the rest of the day cleaning
and organizing the linen cupboard. We ate dinner by
candlelight that night.

The Cumberland house was a peculiar assortment of rooms. My next job was sorting and cleaning all the boxes out of a space right inside the front entrance. I don't remember if Mummy and Daddy told me their plans for the area, but it probably was to be a sewing room for Mummy or a workshop for Daddy. I started splitting the boxes and laying them flat until I picked up one, and a dozen or more large cockroaches fell out—memories flooded my brain. I hated cockroaches as a child when I had to use the outhouse at night. The noise they made as they scuttled across the walls and ceilings was terrifying. I was afraid they would drop and land on me. Even when crunched underfoot, those shiny, three-inch-long, hard-shelled insects were hard to kill. I screamed!

The boxes shot into the air as I fled from the room and ran down the front stairs. I kept walking until I'd calmed down. When I returned, Daddy glanced up at me from his chair and laughed, "No cockroaches left now. You scared them all away with your scream."

"Don't laugh. It's not funny. Those cockroaches were huge."

"I made sure all the boxes were empty and folded for you," he said quietly.

"Thank you. Ugh, horrible creatures," I shuddered visibly.

Mummy's cedar press (hope chest) was in the corner of that space. I remembered it sitting in the front room of my last home—Sunningdale, Calliaqua. Her cut-glass bowl—the last remaining piece of her wedding crystal—sat in the middle of the lid, the tall brass cannon shell casings from WWI on either side. Now, the chest was dusty and sticky with dirt and dead midges. I knew that once I'd cleaned and polished the press, its smell of fragrant red cedar would permeate the room, and the odd, broken-down house might feel like home.

Returning from my walk to calm down, I saw a thick rope in the carport and thought I would make a swing. Leaving the cedar press until the next day, I cut a notch on either side of a short rough board, threw the rope over a rafter to the right of the car, pulled it down, tied a reef knot, pulled the rope back up, and placed the board over the rope. For a short while, I was transported back to being seven years old in Montserrat and making a swing from cardboard and string. How small and light I must have been. It had been one of my safe places back then.

The swing was a nice distraction from the distance I felt from Mummy and Daddy—my childhood was not here. Both my pets were gone. Bingo, the boxer puppy I had since I was ten, had died after an angry person hit him and broke his back before Mummy and Daddy left Calliaqua. Wong, our seal-point siamese who'd been in the family since Montserrat, was gone too—he had eaten the bristles of a hard plastic brush used to clean fish and died from a punctured stomach. Such horrible deaths to my beloved pets; it was hard to keep the sorrow inside.

The sadness of not being here when Mummy and Daddy needed me endured. There was an unspoken pain hovering in the air amongst us. In the five years

I'd had been gone, my world had changed dramatically, and Mummy and Daddy had aged. I had been through so much emotional upheaval that I didn't know how to talk to Mummy anymore. As a child, I was shy and compliant, but the ground beneath my feet was firmly planted in my belief in Mummy and Daddy. Now, I was a quiet teenager in their home. Being practical seemed the only way forward. Cleaning was an easy thing to do.

When I started cleaning out the cedar press, I felt the separation even more harshly. I found a letter written to Mummy from Thea just after I was born; a photo fell out of a pretty woman and a baby. On the back was written, "She's beautiful and she's mine." But the letter was harsh. The words pierced my heart. My birth mother wrote that she tried to abort with horse riding. I had never known that piece of my trauma. I jumped up, tore the letter into pieces, and scattered them to the wind. I wondered why Mummy had kept that letter. It was too painful to ask.

Many years later, I wrote a poem that helped me understand the separation and loss I felt.

Beautiful Baby

A dichotomy of lies
Played out in their lives.

"It's a bastard,
Wish it was dead."
Both survived.

A dichotomy of lies
Played out in their lives.

"She beautiful, and she's mine."
The mother wrote
A baby, wistfully held
Asleep in her arms.

1970
Daddy and the Demon Rum

The New Year brought Daddy's return to his old drinking habits. On the way into town, he'd stop to buy a drink and then again on the way home. The journey into town was always happy with our singing and laughter, but that changed once we reached Kingstown.

Our first stop was just beyond the ornate Catholic church. The first time, Daddy pulled over, stopped the car, and asked me if I wanted a cream soda, a drink I had loved as a child.

"I'll …" I started to say.

Mummy turned quickly in her seat, stopping me with her finger to her lips, "Let him go alone," she mimed.

"I'll stay here, Daddy," I finished saying.

I never knew if Daddy thought we didn't know. When I asked Mummy where he had gone, she replied with unhidden contempt, "To buy his rum." That was the end of the matter, and it was never spoken of between us again or to Daddy.

Daddy wasn't gone long, but he'd had enough
time to buy a drink and bring a small paper bag stuffed
into his back pocket. It contained a nip, a 50 or 100 ml
bottle of rum. There was an uncomfortable silence in
the car until Daddy dropped Mummy and me off at the
post office.

We had to wait for the Black woman behind the
metal grill as she continued to talk to her friends before
she looked for our mail. There had been political unrest
on the island amongst the Whites and Blacks since
the collapse of the West Indies Federation of 1962.
Mummy said the unrest had intensified in recent years
because of the political leaders on the island. It made
Mummy and Daddy uncomfortable in their old age,
afraid for their well-being.

Once we had our mail, we walked to Corea's
General Store to collect our supplies for the next few
days. Daddy, coming from the meat market, picked us
up and took us out to the White House in time for
lunch. Afterwards, Mummy took a nap. As I left to
walk over to the Aquatic Club to meet some friends, I
saw Daddy drink his nip of rum.

At about 3:00 p.m., Daddy picked me up for the
return trip home. The routine was the same. We stopped
on Bay Street just before the marketplace. Daddy got
out, left us in the car for twenty minutes or so, and
returned with another small paper bag sticking out of
his back pocket.

The drive home wasn't fun. Daddy had already
consumed at least three drinks of rum, probably double
shots. The road out of town wound up the hill to Fort

Charlotte and then took a sharp turn before running downhill until it reached a small bridge at the bottom. Daddy had an ardent wish to coast to the bridge and cross it without lifting his clutch foot—thus saving gas. He was confident he could regain control of the car quickly, but it was scary with the car freewheeling down the narrow road.

Mummy sat in the passenger seat, tensely staring straight ahead with her fingers crossed on both hands, her toes too, she told me later. I sat in the back and pretended nothing was unusual. I wanted to scream at Daddy to slow down and be careful. Instead, I prayed silently that we would get home in one piece. Daddy performed this craziness every time we went into town.

On one of our trips home, Daddy had drunk more than usual, and he couldn't complete the final sharp left-hand turn off the main road and the equally quick right turn to park under the house. He made a few abortive attempts before Mummy shouted, "God, damn it, Clem. Let me get out." Exhausted with frustration and worry, she got out and went into the house without looking back, leaving me to deal with Daddy and the car.

I was energized and terrified, being left in charge of Daddy parking the car. I ran from front to back, banging and shouting, first on the bonnet, then on the boot, to make him stop before he drove or reversed over the edge of the fifty-foot drop into the abyss of the forest. Finally, he parked, and I went inside. Mummy was stretched out on her bed, asleep.

After I returned to England, Mummy wrote in her

letters that Daddy continued to drink and try to make the bridge with the engine off until they moved back into town in 1971. They stayed at Arnos Vale House, the home of Daddy's sister, and began preparations for returning to England.

Just before they left the island, Daddy fell and cracked a few ribs on a boot scraper at the house. Ironically, he wasn't drunk at the time, but his doctor bandaged him so tightly that he nearly had a heart attack, which scared him. Daddy never drank the demon rum again.

Mummy and Daddy moved to England to live with their two oldest daughters, Anne and Lorna, who, together, bought a big house in Devon. There, Daddy became a "jolly, roly-poly man" with a bright red laughing face, whom all his grandchildren loved. Sometimes, Daddy went down to the pub a few doors from their house. He'd nurse a pint of beer for a few hours and grumble amicably to anyone who'd listen about being the only man in a house full of women— his wife and two daughters.

Three Weeks on *The Age of Aquarius*

In the New Year, I was excited when Mummy introduced me to some people who took care of yachts for wealthy American owners. Her words still carried weight on the island. "Working for them will be a great way to earn my airfare back to England," I wrote to William.

Towards the end of February, I took a boat to Port Elizabeth, Bequia, to meet the American East Coast owners of the *Age of Aquarius*, a fifty-five-foot schooner. We drove out to Friendship Bay to meet the other crew members, two boys sailing their way around the world, and sailed back to St. Vincent that evening to pick up another couple and the supplies for the nine people sailing together in the fifty-five-foot moving space! I would be the cook—something I had never done before. It would be a new adventure.

We sailed back to Bequia the following morning in time for lunch. It is the second largest island in the Grenadines, a beautiful place with great anchorage, accessible only by boat in the 1960s. We moored in the crystal-clear waters of Port Elizabeth and went ashore. My memory still holds one impression of that day— sitting on a stool in the sand, eating lobster. I had never tried lobster before. The pure, unadulterated, sweet flesh filled my mouth and mind—no lobster since has tasted as good. We stayed a second night in the harbour before slipping quietly away in the early morning, just as the sun rose warmly over the horizon.

Our second stop was a small island off Bequia called Petite St. Vincent, a whaling station where they still caught whales using a long boat and hand-held harpoons.

We stopped to watch the ceremony of the division of the whale meat amongst the islanders. In a letter home to William, I wrote:

> *It was a sight to see, the sea scarlet with blood, people everywhere. The meat belongs to the whalers and their family members and is cut*

*up and divided. They, in turn, share with their
families and friends until everyone has a piece
of the catch. Even the youngest child is playing
in the blood, while the older ones fight to be the
first to be given the first piece of blubber. The
women cook and salt the meat on the beach,
and the offal that isn't used is dumped back in
the sea some distance from the shore to keep the
sharks away from the beach.*

The boy I liked the most, fought with one of the owners and left. The argument appeared to be about one of the wives. Mummy would have called her, "A bit of a flirt, just after a good time." The young man, whose name I don't remember, didn't want to play her game.

Unfortunately, from my young perspective, the new person they brought on board, Mike, was a creep because he walked around the boat in his underwear. He might have done it to embarrass me, as I was quiet and shy, but I felt uncomfortable with his behaviour because I had to share the V-shaped foc'sle berth with both boys. I slept in the middle on the short mattress while the boys slept on either side, against the inside of the bow—it was a longer space. I was grateful when they both opted to sleep on deck.

The clear and deep turquoise water around the Grenadine Islands was incredible, a tropical paradise. I loved the vivid colours of the fish in the shallow water. In the deeper water, there were flying fish and leaping dolphins. There were no airports on the small islands; access was only by fishing or sailboats. Only a couple of the islands had vehicular traffic and none we visited until we reached Grenada.

Canouan is a 3.5 square mile island in the Caribbean archipelago of the nation of St.Vincent and the Grenadines, known for its beautiful, fine white sandy beaches and towering Mount Royal. After an arduous climb, I sat on the flat rock at the top, looking out on a fantastic panoramic view of the islands: Mayreau, Union Island, Carriacou, and Petit St.Vincent. I would have liked to sit and look out over the peaceful and tranquil scene alone. Instead, I had to endure the noisy chatter of the others.

We stopped at Union Island briefly. It became known as the Gateway to the Tobago Cays and was always a favourite anchor spot for cruising sailboats. While the rest of the crew and owners spent their time sitting in the hotel bar, I walked along the beach. I loved the feel of the hot sand beneath my feet. The ground gradually changed from soft sand to broken conch shells. At first, I didn't realise the change because they were ground smoothly into tiny pieces, but the further I walked away from the anchorage spot, the bigger the shells became until the beach was all shells. I was glad I had brought my sand shoes with me as the broken shells were sharp.*

We finished the cruise in Grenada, and the owners returned to New York. We stayed moored for another week, undergoing minor repairs—something to do with

*An interesting aside: There is a tiny atoll called Happy Island, a few hundred metres off Union Island, made entirely of conch shells and owned by Janti, a former volunteer environmental officer. He collected the discarded shells to create his island and built a bar. It opened to the public in 2002. Today, the bar is famous throughout the Caribbean.

the bilge and the alternator. The pump was choked with hundreds of paper dollars floating in the stagnant water. Neither of the boys seemed to know how the money came to be there. I would have liked to pick up many of those bills, but the water was nasty. I left the guys to work alone, thinking if they wanted the money, they were welcome to take it. I enjoyed touring the island instead.

One of my strongest memories of Grenada was meeting a young woman sailing around the world with her husband and a beautiful, curly-haired, blonde toddler. I was fascinated by the hair on the lady's legs, tiny semi-circle curls of golden hair laying flat against her rich, sun-browned skin. That memory would return many times, bringing a smile to my face.

The highlight of the three-week cruise, during which I prepared only half a dozen meals, was the journey back to St. Vincent when we encountered a force nine squall. The boys managed the schooner, which heeled to port and raced with the wind. My memory still recalls the feeling of the enormous swells of the dark sea rising and rolling beneath the boat. With the sails reefed and tied to the mast, a rope secured around my waist, the wind whipped my hair, and the salty water swirled knee-deep around my legs as I cleaned the flying fish we had caught earlier. I wasn't afraid; in fact, I felt I was in heaven. When I looked up, I saw dolphins racing alongside us and leaping across our bow.

I left the *Age of Aquarius* when we returned to Bequia and joined another small sailing boat before returning to St. Vincent. I probably asked the boys to deliver a letter to Mummy and Daddy letting them know my new plans. The owner of the second boat was an older English gentleman who, although I didn't realise it at the time, was a multi-millionaire in steel. He had businesses in Australia, Canada, and England and wanted to start a fleet of small boats in the Caribbean. This was his maiden cruise to check out the viability of the venture.

I was having a wonderful time; the man was knowledgeable and kind. We enjoyed the days together and went to our separate cabins at night. All went well until the day a young boy, diving for pennies, asked, "Is dat your missus?"

He answered, "Yes, this lady's my wife."

I'm sure he meant well but his reply freaked me out. I wanted to get off the boat as soon as possible. I wasn't and didn't want to be married to a man so much older than me. I sometimes wonder what I would be doing now if I had taken the job of managing a fleet of small charter boats or married him. It might have been a good life. Instead, I returned to England and married William.

Enjoying the Teenage Life

I went on a spending spree while in Grenada on the *Age of Aquarius*. I bought two folk-embroidered Hungarian blouses, a lovely sky-blue, two-piece bell-bottom outfit, and two bikinis—they made me feel bold and pretty, and they were all the rage.

Back home, Mummy helped me make another dress for a Saturday night dance. It was beautiful, ankle-length, with a mandarin collar cut from a dark blue patterned silk. It was split up one side to under the armhole and had tiny material-covered buttons with loops down to the mid-thigh. That night, I wore my hair in curls piled high on my head and gold high-heeled sandals.

On one occasion, at the Aquatic Club, I met a man whose name I cannot remember; I'll call him Samuel. He was new in town, from Trinidad, he said. I hadn't seen him before. After spending a short time on the beach, I was ready to go home, but he wouldn't stop asking me to go to the Saturday night dance with him. It didn't matter how often I said, "No thanks, I'm going with a friend." Eventually, I reluctantly agreed.

"I was kinda afraid to say no in the end," I told Mummy. "He kept badgering me to say yes, which was annoying. I only said yes to shut him up so I could come home. I'm going with Andrew. The annoying man's name is Samuel—will you tell him I'm sick?" I asked.

When the man came to the house, Mummy told him I had a headache and couldn't go with him to the dance. I don't remember thinking Mummy and Daddy were quite so liberal, but looking back, I was surprised by their reactions.

Andrew picked me up at the White House, and while we were having a wonderful time dancing, I felt a tap on my shoulder. The man I'd turned down was standing there smiling at me. I felt intensely embarrassed, wanting to disappear into the ground. Fortunately, Samuel was polite and understanding.

Andrew was very different from any other man I'd known. He was confident, a good dancer, and an easy talker. He was also suave and a good kisser. I was still very naive and knew nothing about contraceptives. I also believed in loyalty. If it hadn't been for William back in England, I might have stayed in St. Vincent.

I met Hammed at the Aquatic Club, a beautiful, seductive-looking man. As I exited the shower room, he was lying on a beach towel a few feet away. Our eyes met, and he smiled. I stopped, captivated by his smile, and we chatted for a while before he asked if I'd like to go on an evening picnic. "That would be lovely," I said. "But I live out at Cumberland and don't drive."

"I'll come and pick you up, he replied. There is a lovely beach out there."

When Hammed arrived at our house, he called Daddy "Pops." I held my breath, expecting Daddy to explode, but after a slight pause, he said, "Have a good evening, and make sure you bring my girl back in one piece."

"Okay. Will do, sir," Hammed replied with a big smile, showing two rows of perfectly white teeth.

"I'll see you in the morning," I said as we left, the picnic basket over Hammed's arm. Mummy had packed a couple of meat pies and her special eggless chocolate cake.

Mummy looked up from peeling potatoes at the kitchen sink and smiled. Daddy lowered his newspaper and winked, "Have fun, Janie."

When we got into the car, Hammed leaned into the back and tossed two cans of Dr Peppers into the picnic basket. "We'll take these as well."

The beach glowed in perfect moonlight and the sea lapped the shore with a quiet melody. I was excited, being out on the beach alone with this incredibly handsome man. I laid out the blanket on the still-warm sand and started lifting the food from the basket before I discovered to my dismay, that food was the last thing on Hammed's mind.

I wriggled out of his arms, muttering, "I'm sorry … I've never … I'd rather not … I don't want to … I want to wait … " I felt my face burning as I stammered incoherently.

Hammed put his thumb and first finger under my chin and lifted my face to his, "An innocent eh? You'll be all right, don't worry. I promised your Pops, didn't I? Let's eat a little of your mother's food."

I was a bit scared, especially when I noticed a small pistol in his shirt pocket as he raised my face to his, But he never touched me again. We drank the Dr Peppers and ate a little of the cake before Hammed suggested taking me home.

I sank into bed that night, relieved yet emotionally excited by the experience. I saw Hammed once more before I left the island, sitting on a bar stool in the Aquatic Club when I walked through. He smiled and winked, making me blush from the tip of my head to my toes.

After that incident, I played it safe and went out with a pleasant younger man called Stephen. We had a lot of fun. We went rowing in a glass-bottom boat and climbed Fort Duvernette—the 190-foot volcanic rock I once swam to. We walked on the beach and went dancing in the evening. I enjoyed the time we spent together. He liked my company, and I didn't have to hold him at arm's length. We enjoyed a simple goodnight kiss when we parted, and were happy to see each other the next day. But on our last evening together, Stephen became emotionally and sexually aroused, which spoilt the evening and changed how I felt about him. I was ready to go home. I flew back to Barbados and, after a short stay with Douglas and family, on to England.

I have many questions about those three months back in St. Vincent, which were never answered. Why did Mummy and I not talk about my time in England? Was it stoicism? Self-control on both our parts to avoid destructive emotions? Why did Mummy and Daddy never ask me questions when I went out with different men? Did Mummy trust and believe in me to do the right things? Had she questioned Thea, when she went out with young men? Did she believe I would go the way of my birth mother, and she could only hope and pray? I did have one advantage, which Mummy never mentioned either: I did not smoke or drink and, therefore, wouldn't be caught with a Mickey Finn,* like Thea when she was my age.

*A drink laced with an incapacitating drug, usually chloral hydrate.

1970
Return to England

I remember very little about my return to England. In re-reading letters I wrote to William, it appeared that my plans changed a few times. At first, I intended to take the Geest boat to Barry in Wales. I wanted to relive the joy of being on board a banana boat, the same as I had done when I was fourteen. Then I had a couple of flights lined up. In the end, Douglas paid for me to fly on BOAC, possibly on a VC10, after he had given up trying to persuade me to stay and live with them.

The flight was definitely superior to my West Indian charter flight from England. There was more room, and we were given a great meal and plenty of snacks. The only item that wasn't good was the warm Coca-Cola. It reminded me that I was leaving the tropics. I felt sad, realizing I was leaving a part of me behind, probably forever.

William and I had written letters to each other in the months I was away, which helped bridge the gap in the physical affection we had shared. I read in his letters that he missed me and was looking forward to my return. I was delighted to read at the end of his last letter:

> *. . . I've dreamt of your coming back and seen*
> *you running down the platform in a dress, or*
> *in trousers, dragging your suitcase or swinging*

*it over your head, in fact I've already met you
quite a number of times, I look forward to the
last.*

It would not be the same as when I first arrived
in England in 1964—six years had passed since then.
I wasn't a lonely child anymore. I believed everything
would be different this time. I was choosing to come
back. In the three months I was away, I had grown
emotionally and physically. My hair was blonde with
a beautiful cut, and my skin tanned a golden brown
because whenever I had the chance, I slathered olive oil
on my body and laid out in the sun.

I remembered writing to Thea, asking if I could
stay for a few weeks, and she'd said yes. I would
be looking for a flat (apartment) or shared living
conditions near where I worked as soon as possible. I
found in my letters to William that I had a re-starting
date of June 1st at my old job at Mullards in Salfords.
I do not recall what it was like going back to work.
I'm sure I took little gifts for all the girls and women I
worked with in the "Clean Room."

William was disappointed because he couldn't meet
me. He had planned on taking time off work, but with
all the changes in my flights, he was in Belgium when
I arrived. I do not recall who picked me up or whether
I had to find my own way back to the corner house in
Pound Hill.

Although I did not move into a flat as quickly
as I would have liked, it was apparent from a few of
William's letters that he was looking for places for me.

Rent was between £3 and £5 a week. Thea was initially pleased to have me living at home, but I still didn't fit in.

Now I was back, William had to relinquish my green Lambretta scooter he'd been using while I was in St. Vincent. He'd written saying he was considering not returning it. "Over my dead body," I wrote back. He never mentioned using it again until after we were married.

During the summer of 1970, William and I went on a week's holiday to Hastings. On one of the days, we came across a lovely pottery studio. After touring the place, William said, "Maybe we could buy six of these pretty blue bowls?"

I was pleasantly surprised. Unfortunately, I didn't understand that this suggestion was a marriage proposal. I never did well with indirect questions. Later, after dinner at our bed and breakfast place, William said he was waiting for a reply. "To what?" I asked.

"The bowls," he said in a slightly shocked voice. "They'll be nice to serve soup or dessert to our friends, don't you agree?"

"I think they are beautiful, but we don't have a home to put them in."

William turned my face to look at him. I saw that his eyes had turned bright blue. He smiled, "Darling, don't you understand why I bought the bowls? We'll get our own home very soon."

A few tears and cuddles followed as we lay on my bed at the bed and breakfast, surrounded by tissue paper and bowls. I had known William and his family for a long time, and I thought being with him would complete me. I remember thinking, *William doesn't make me laugh, but that's no big deal. I don't laugh much anyway, not since leaving Mummy and Daddy.* I believed marriage would finally give me a sense of belonging I had not felt in the last six years. I had always felt the odd one out, the stranger amid the family, and after three months in St. Vincent and Barbados, I found I no longer fit into that culture either.

I reasoned that William wasn't a particularly emotional man, and his humour was definitely not the same as mine. But I loved that he was quiet, didn't drink or smoke, and didn't go out with the boys as many of my friends' boyfriends did. He liked many things I enjoyed and didn't make demands of me that I was uncomfortable with. At least, that was true until we were married.

Mummy and Daddy in their garden on St.
Vincent, 1970.

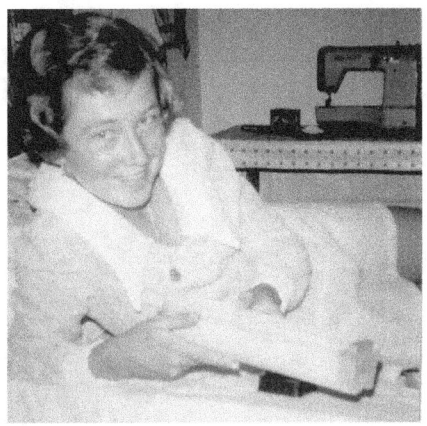

Jane in the house in Barbados.

Jane and Uncle Douglas.

Jane and her cousins. Left to right: Dörn, Jane, Timothy, and Rafé

The White House in Kingstown,
St. Vincent.

Jane, in the gold lamé
dress that Mummy
helped Jane cut out
and sew.

Jane in the forefront with *The Age of Aquarius*,
the sailboat for which she was hired as a cook, in
the background.

On the small island of Petite St. Vincent, a whaling
station, the *Age of Aquarius* stopped to view a ceremony
where whale meat was distributed among family, 1970.

Bikini day on Diamond Beach,
St. Vincent

Jane posing on a rock on St. Vincent, an island
in the eastern Caribbean. 1970.

Marriage

A Well-behaved Couple

As requested, William wrote to Daddy for my hand in marriage—a courtesy I knew he would love.

> *Dear William,*
>
> *Both Mrs. Moller and I were very pleased to receive your letter of 18th August wherein you request the hand of our daughter Jane, in marriage . . . we have no hesitation in accepting you as yet another son–in–law and considering the present day casual approach to marriage your courtesy is appreciated . . . God bless you both!*
>
> *On behalf of Mrs. Moller and myself,*
> *Yours sincerely,*
> *Clement Moller.*

After the approval letter arrived, William and I went looking for an engagement ring together. We toured the antique shops of East Grinstead and Redhill. We were looking for something unusual and not too expensive. We found it in Redhill, in a tiny, dirty-looking corner shop. It was the perfect ring—old gold with a three-diamond set in what the jeweller called a balanced setting. Unfortunately, a few weeks later, one of the diamonds fell out. The jeweller was willing to exchange the ring for another one. This time, I chose a ruby set in the middle of a cluster of three tiny diamonds with a much tighter setting. Later, I found the lost diamond and had it put into a plain gold wedding band for William.

The following Saturday, William and I went into Crawley. We wandered around the stores as an engaged couple, we bought an expensive, yellow-handled, double-edged potato peeler—it felt silly but romantic. Afterwards, we went to Graham's house to tell him about our engagement. Unfortunately, it made me late home for dinner that evening in the corner house.

On Sunday, William and I went to Worth together—it was my family church. After the service, we talked to Father Nicholas about booking a wedding. He was a sweet, elderly priest I had known for a long time, and therefore expected counsel from him, but William was surprised when Father Nicholas reminded us that fornication was a sin in the eyes of God. William was a non-believer but was prepared to be married in the church for my sake.

We initially picked a date just after Easter but discovered that everything was twice as expensive after the holiday. We couldn't be married during Lent, so we settled on Saturday, February 12th, four days before Ash Wednesday.

After talking with Father Nicholas, William and I walked back to his parent's house to tell June, Bill, his brother Christopher, and his sister Susan about the wedding date—it was exciting. June offered to make the dresses for the wedding. I would have two bridesmaids, Susan and my sister Tina. William asked Christopher to be his best man.

Spending time with William's family caused me to arrive home late for dinner again. Thea was furious. She refused to listen to where I had been and what I had spent the weekend doing. Tina was sixteen and pleased to be asked to be a bridesmaid, but the argument with Thea muted our excitement.

William and I arranged an engagement party for October to coincide with my twenty-first birthday at a reception hall in East Grinstead. Brian, my friend Linda's brother, was a baker and made our cake. It was beautiful, with royal icing lattice filigree work around the sides and flowers on the top. Both families attended the celebration, including mine and William's friends from work. We all had a wonderful time. I wore the dark blue mandarin dress I had made with Mummy in St. Vincent.

It was very late when William and I finished cleaning up. I decided that at two in the morning, it was too late to bicycle another hour back to the corner house in the damp mist that hung over Copthorne Common. I spent the night at William's tiny flat, sleeping on a mattress on the floor. When I arrived at the house about lunchtime the next day, Thea and Don assumed I had slept with William. Once again, I was not believed for telling the truth. My five-year-old sister, Sophie, obviously following up on the overheard conversations, came upstairs to question me on my whereabouts the night before. As Mummy would have said, "It was the straw that broke the camel's back." Any good feelings between Thea and me broke completely. During the next two weeks, I packed up my stuff, and

William helped me move into his cousin Stephanie's home in Northgate.

We were both young people who believed in doing things in the correct order. Now that we were engaged, I went to my doctor to ask about birth control pills. Before prescribing them, my doctor had a series of questions about my monthly menstruation: "How heavy was the bleeding? How long did I bleed? Did I have pain before, during, or after menstruation?" Then he asked, "Any pain after intercourse?"

At first, I answered automatically, "No," without thinking about the context of his question. Then I stopped, turned bright red, and said, "I don't know, I haven't had . . . I thought it best to go on the pill first. We will be getting married in a few months."

Now, it was the doctor's turn to be embarrassed, "Oh! Umm . . . Oh dear, umm, I won't be able to examine you, will I? Well, I think you are healthy enough, my dear. I'll prescribe a low-dose pill, and you can let me know if you suffer any problems. You can start these seven days after the beginning of your next period, and you should wait for at least one full cycle afterwards before having intercourse."

"Thank you," I muttered, and still bright red in the face, I left the doctor's office.

We were good, waiting the required six weeks, but we talked of little else during that time. We decided that this pivotal moment in our lives should happen in my bed at William's cousin's house when we knew Stephanie would be out with the children for a few hours. It worked perfectly. Our coupling was short, sweet, and incomplete, but I can still remember the joy and thrill of that experience. I wanted to savour the romantic moment forever, at least longer than William wanted to.

Next, we scoured the newspapers for a flat. Eventually, we found an upstairs place in West Hoathly, which had the use of a large portion of a shared garden. It was a lovely, clean place near East Grinstead, where William worked. I would have much further to travel to work, but William said with a smile, "You have the Lambretta."

I lived in the flat for about two months before we were married. William gave up his flat in East Grinstead and moved in about a month after me but didn't inform his parents that I would also be there. One day, they came to visit unexpectedly. We were in a panic, hastily agreeing that I should hide in a large overhead kitchen cupboard. William boosted me up, and I crawled in and turned around, wedging myself in, and pulled the cupboard door shut as William answered the front door. I heard him tell his mother he had been in the loo to her query, "What took you so long to answer the door?" All was well until June started looking for cups to make tea. I held on tightly to the inside latch as she tugged at the cupboard door.

"Mum! Not that cupboard. I have the cups and saucers here."

"It's stuck anyway," June answered. "Do you want your Dad to look at it? He could fix it for you."

"No, no, it's okay. Let's take our tea out to the garden, and you can give me some ideas to tell Jane."

I opened the cupboard door and breathed a sigh of relief as they went down the stairs and outside. I was sweaty, stiff, and glad William had suggested they went into the garden. I climbed out and went into our bedroom, which they'd seen already. I didn't think they would come into the house again.

"That was close. I thought my parents would never leave," William said when he came upstairs.

It's My Right

L ooking back, I don't believe William and I were consciously aware of the political tensions between Ireland and England. But I'm sure we were subconsciously affected by the upheaval in the news over the couple of months surrounding our wedding. I am surprised at the small details I remember and how completely I have forgotten other parts of the day.

January 30th is known as Bloody Sunday in Northern Ireland. British troops had killed fourteen unarmed civilian Catholics in Derry. Some of the events were close to home, such as the bombing of the Aldershot Barracks—a familiar place I'd been with Don and his army cadets. Also, my brother Derek narrowly escaped two bombings in Central London. I vaguely remember that Irish protesters burnt down the British Embassy in Dublin. On top of all these terrible acts of violence, England was under a state of emergency, called for by Prime Minister Edward Heath on February 9th because of the miner's strike. It started in the first week of January 1972 and lasted for seven weeks, ending on February 25th.

I woke alone, around 7: 00 a.m. on the morning of our wedding. I felt slightly disorientated, looking around the darkened room and wondering why this day was different. Then I remembered—I'm getting married.

I leisurely got out of bed, changed the linens, cleaned, and opened all the windows to let in "a breath of fresh air," as Mummy would have said. I closed them again later, along with the curtains, to keep in the heat, which came from large storage heaters, a popular, less expensive form of electricity that used night-time power to store heat and release it during the day. Unfortunately, by early afternoon, the flat cooled down. Closing the curtains helped keep the rooms warm. I didn't want us to be cold when we arrived later that evening.

I wrapped a small gift for William in blue and silver paper, tied it with a striped red ribbon, and placed it on the small table on his side of the bed. I took the new pajamas and nightdress I had bought for us out of the packaging and laid them on the bed. I remember standing back and being excited at the thoughts of a romantic evening. After I was done, I took a cool bath and waited for the taxi I'd ordered to take me to Three Bridges to have my hair done. Looking back, I discovered a strange loss of memory from that point until I reached the church door.

Sophie, who was only seven years old then, told me recently that Mummy and Daddy, who had been in England for only a few weeks, were staying with Mrs. Ridgeway, the neighbour. I do not remember where my bridesmaids, Tina and Susan, dressed, where we met, or how they got to the church. It would make sense that I dressed at Mrs. Ridgeway's house and then left in a car with Daddy. I do remember that Mummy was quite ill at the time. I have since asked Thea and Tina, but neither have filled in the blanks in my memory.

With a state of emergency in the country and the uncertainty of available electricity, which was cut several times a day, I thought it a good omen that as I approached the main doors of Worth Church, the electricity was restored. I walked down the aisle on Daddy's arm to the sound of the organ playing Wagner's Wedding March to stand next to William in front of the oldest Saxon arch in England.

Our reception was held in the home of William's grandparents, Fred and Rose Welby. Nan, as everyone called her, and her daughter, June, my mother-in-law, prepared a wonderful sit-down meal. We had Martinelli's apple cider for the toast and a beautiful wedding cake made by Brian Tobin.

Looking at my wedding album, I see Thea and Don's names written in the guest list, but I only see Don in the group photo. If they came to our reception, I do not recall since no pictures were taken during that time. I remember Mummy refusing even a sip of the cider—she only drank water or tea. After the toast and cutting the cake, Mummy and Daddy left. The tables and chairs were cleared away, and the party began. It was so wonderful that I didn't want to say goodbye. But, eventually, just after ten o'clock that night, we got into William's green Hillman Imp and drove away to cheers and laughter. We would fly to Majorca on Monday for a four-day honeymoon in the sunshine.

Bill, William's dad, picked us up on Monday morning and dropped us off at Gatwick Airport for our short flight to Majorca. Memory is sporadic, but I do recall our confusion when the cleaning crew kept separating our beds every morning. I remember a horse-drawn carriage ride around the town, drinking inexpensive wine late at night, and then not being able to get water from the hotel kitchen.

I became so desperate for water that I stood under the shower and drank, even though we were told not to. The combination of sex, cheap wine, and lack of clean water resulted in me getting a severe urinary infection. In pain and unable to see a doctor for a few days, we had our first major upset the night we got home. William wanted sex, but I didn't. He sulked, and I cried. It was a shock hearing the man I loved and had never made demands of me before saying, "It's my right."

We had no role models for this stumbling block. William didn't show his emotions, and I never told him how hurt I'd felt. I had been taught to accept that I was my husband's wife. Neither of us understood that our lack of communication was a serious problem we should have discussed. Nor did we seek counsel or speak about the incident again. I never threw it back at William, but my trust was broken, which wrecked the foundation of our marriage. I never fully forgot the emotional and physical pain that incident caused—it was always in the back of my mind.

1972–1973
West Hoathly

Our First Home

West Hoathly, our first home, is a small village with an ancient history, nestled in the High Weald near the medieval market town of East Grinstead. The village was established by Norman settlers in the forest near the sand and limestone quarries. Although not mentioned in the Doomsday Survey of 1086, there is evidence that a simple church existed in 1090.*

We chose the flat not for its location or history but because it was a large, comfortable, upstairs converted space with a lovely view and a reasonable rent. We paid £36 a month. The population of West Hoathly was 2,181 in 2011. It was even smaller when we lived there.

Four ancient buildings from medieval times still exist today: The Cat Inn**—the present building originates from around 1690. St Margaret's Church— built by the Normans in the eleventh century. The Gravetye Manor***—now a one-star Michelin hotel and restaurant—was built for love in 1598 by Richard Infield as a gift for his bride, Katharine Compton. This serene 16th-century manor house is surrounded by a thousand acres of stunning gardens and forests. I knew of the Priest House****—originally built as a Hall House with a central hearth, but neither of us ever made it inside while we lived in our flat. We got up in the mornings, went to work, came home, ate, and slept.

*https://en.wikipedia.org/wiki/St_Margaret's_Church,_West_Hoathly
**thecatinn.co.uk

*** https://www.gravetyemanor.co.uk
**** https://en.wikipedia.org/wiki/The_Priest_House,_West_Hoathly

Sadly, we were oblivious to all this history surrounding us.

William, who wanted to become an artist, began painting a large canvas of one of the trails on the property we sometimes walked along. The bottom left-hand corner of that painting, which William cut and framed, still hangs in my bedroom. I have kept it as a reminder of how much William loved painting.

On weekends, I visited Thea at the corner house for an hour. I mainly sat in silence with a cup of tea. I knew Thea's life wasn't easy, but our hurt feelings created a barrier to conversation. Going to visit was my way of showing I cared.

We had been living in the flat for less than a month when we received a visit from a neighbour. She introduced herself but immediately began to upbraid us for not opening our curtains during the day. "It is unhealthy," she counseled.

I was flabbergasted. Why was a total stranger telling us how to live our lives? I started to explain about the heaters, but William cut me off. "Please mind your own business, and don't interfere with us again."

While I cleared the garden of weeds and planted potatoes, I occasionally saw that neighbour painting in her garden. Sometimes, we would wave. I could tell that her paintings were vibrant and colourful. Her artwork was featured in an art exhibition held at the church later that summer. I remember being shocked due to my upbringing. I felt they were vulgar and inappropriate for a church setting. They were abstract nudes painted with heavy brush strokes and bright shades of red, orange, and yellow, accented by flashes of blue. The only other time I remember seeing this colourful lady was early one morning when I opened the living room curtains and saw her singing and dancing in her garden, completely naked! Back then, I thought she must be crazy, but now I look back and admire her freedom of expression. William's reaction was to say, "She's not right in the head."

One evening, while I was sitting on the sofa in the living room reading, there was a loud explosion. Before I could react, a cascade of creamy, bubbling froth spilled from the bottom of the sideboard doors. I shrieked and then laughed; William had forgotten to release the pressure that had built up in his bottles of homemade ginger beer over a couple of days. A flurry of activity ensued as William ran from the bedroom while I grabbed all the towels we owned. He attempted to save a few bottles as I mopped up the sticky mess on the carpet.

William moved on to wine. He made the best blackberry wine that year with the fruit picked on the estate of Gravetye Manor. He also made white wine from the discarded pea-pod shells from his mother. We hardly noticed the big white plastic buckets in the living room. When William bottled the wine, we ended up with them lining the hallway from the top of the stairs, avoiding the entrances to the bathroom and bedroom, and continuing around into the living room. Neither of us thought it odd until a service man came to deliver a washing machine. I have never forgotten the startled look in the man's eyes after he had struggled up the long flight of stairs and saw all those bottles around the space. William and I laughed that evening, wondering what he might have told his wife when he'd gone home. "I'm sure it made his day," William said.

While we lived in West Hoathly, I enrolled in a course to take my advanced level English at Crawley Polytechnic. I went straight from work to the college on the Lambretta; occasionally, I would stop by William's parents and have dinner first. One night, when the evenings were darker, I left the college and started the bike. The engine started straight away as usual, but when I turned on the headlight, it died. I did this a couple of times before I gave up and began pushing it the two miles to June and Bill's house. Fortunately, one of my fellow students saw me and offered to ride alongside and share the light from his headlamp. The arrangement worked well. He said goodbye, and I went into the house and talked to Bill. I was tired, frustrated, and hungry and asked if he could drive me home. "Then I can get a lift from work tomorrow and ride home in the daylight."

Bill replied, "Sorry, no can do, I'm just about to go to bed."

But he added a large torch (flashlight) to the handlebars with a bungee cord. This would give me sufficient light for the ride home. I was disappointed. It took at least forty minutes to an hour to make the journey in the daytime, but in the dark unlit streets, it could take longer. I set off, upset, afraid, and with a throbbing head because as Bill had tied the torch to the bike, the bungee had slipped from his fingers and hit me squarely between the eyes. To add to my frustration, my line of vision was compromised by the attached light.

Once I passed through Turners Hill, the road ran through thick woods. I was doing fine, moving slowly and staring ahead through the yellow glow of the torch. Not used to driving without my headlight, I forgot about the sharp corner on Imberhorne Lane and continued straight ahead—I left the paved road and found myself on a trail in the woods.

By this time, I was crying uncontrollably, but I did find my way out of the woods, back onto the road and home. William made me a cup of tea and something to eat, but he didn't understand how traumatised I'd felt.

It turned out that William had caused the problem; in his eagerness to fix the Lambretta, he'd cross-wired the ignition and the headlight. He would commit two similar snafus on our car in the future, one of which caused an interesting drive up to Newcastle with our two small children.

In the seventies, milk was delivered in glass bottles. The milkmen in the towns and cities wore dark blue pants, a jacket, and a peaked cap. They drove three-wheeled red and white milk floats (carts). But our milkman wore brown overalls and a cloth cap. He left us one bottle of "silver-top," full-fat milk unless we left a note under the empties for a second one. We rarely saw him because he came early in the morning while we were still asleep. We only saw him twice, and both times were remarkable. The first time, a friend, who stayed overnight, went to catch the bus to East Grinstead and discovered that either she'd missed it, or it was delayed.

As we stood outside the flat wondering what to do, the mailman stopped the milk float, doffed his cap, and asked, "What's wrong, my dears? Can I help?"

We told him our story. He turned to my friend and said, "I'm done with my deliveries for today, so hop up, dearie, and I'll take you to a place where you'll be in time for the next bus coming in from a different direction." With the innocence of the times, my friend accepted, and I watched with a smile as they rattled up the street.

The next time, we were moving out of the flat. Homeowners usually left a tip for their milkman at Christmastime, but we were moving to our new home in Crawley before the holiday. We left him a couple of pounds in an envelope tucked into the top of the empty milk bottle. Because we were up early and the curtains open, I recognised the little pixie-like man in brown overalls and a cloth cap dancing around his cart, waving our thank-you note.

1973–1978
Crawley

Oulton Walk

By 1973, we were looking to buy a house. The market value for a three-bedroom was around £12,000, and the bank was only prepared to give us a mortgage of £6,000. We had savings of £2,000, but it was not enough. We had almost given up when Nan and Granddad called us.

William's grandparents rented a council home on Oulton Walk, Furnace Green. As secure tenants who had lived in the house for over three years, they were offered the Right to Buy.* They told us, "We are going to emigrate to Australia. We want to spend time with Denise, our youngest daughter, and her new family."

Nan and Granddad suggested that if we acted as guarantors, we could purchase their house. (On paper, if the renters defaulted, we would pay the monies still owing.) We'd have to live in the house for three years or lose the discount. It was an incredible deal, our first home for £7,900, with a mortgage of £6,000. It was our first step on the housing ladder!

The solicitor dealing with our purchase was a large, arrogant man who, I thought, looked down on us. We were the dust under his feet, especially my husband, because he stammered. The man made a mistake in underestimating me. I requested that he write down the costs for each procedure in that first meeting. When it came time to pay him, I discovered he had charged us

---

*Right to Buy: County councils could sell the houses to their tenants since the Housing Act of 1936.

for unregistered land versus registered land,** making the cost considerably higher.

But I had done my homework. The experience of creating the portfolio for building or buying a house for my Duke of Edinburgh Award was very advantageous. The solicitor tried to argue that he hadn't made a mistake until I produced the scrap of paper on which he had written the expenses down. It was an empowering moment.

Our new home, number seven, Oulton Walk, was a three-bedroom house in a high-density block. The residents jokingly referred to it as the "penitentiary." There were long rows of light grey buildings, with ten feet of space between the back fence of one row of houses and the front door of the next row. A wooden fence and a shed on one side divided the houses. There was a tiny patch of garden on either side of the front doors, no grass, and concrete walkways between the houses.

Living in Crawley made travelling to work much easier for us. I rode my bike on good days or the train from Three Bridges to Salfords on rainy days then walked from the station to Mullards. I was part of a team working in a research laboratory for the development of integrated circuits. William had a longer journey as he worked in London at the Royal Marsden Hospital. The cost of rail travel to London and

---

**Around fifteen percent of the land in England and Wales is unregistered: it has an owner, but the details are not registered at the Land Registry. Instead, they are held in private records and likely owned by the same family or institution for decades. This land generally belongs to wealthy families, old institutions, the Church, or the Crown.

back was mitigated by the Inner London weighting, an additional twenty percent cost-of-living allowance on top of William's basic salary.

Before we had children, William bought me a Seal Point Siamese kitten, whom we called Thani. I was delighted; the kitten soothed the ache for Wong, my childhood cat. The antics of the kitten gave us plenty to laugh at. It was a welcome break from spending most of my evenings alone while William was upstairs, studying for his degree with the Open University, a distance-learning course. He felt more secure with me at home, but for me, it was lonely.

We only had one problem with Thani: an infestation of fleas. It was a life-learning lesson—be prepared. Mummy always said, "An ounce of prevention is better than a pound of cure." I came home one evening from work and was instantly covered in fleas. I rushed to the local store and bought three or four cans of flea bombs and took care of the problem before William came home.

A recession followed the 1973 oil crisis. The public spending deficit was the main contributor to the climbing interest rates. In May 1974, exactly a year before my first child was born, my sister Anne's husband, Gerry, was killed in a horrible head-on car collision. He was the passenger in a car going too fast on the A358 near Chard. His suitcase in the back seat flew forward, decapitating him. Even when I learnt to drive many years later, I would avoid that part of the country.

My relationship with Thea improved while I was pregnant; she seemed to understand that I didn't want someone to hold my hand, metaphorically speaking, but was willing to help me with jobs that needed doing. I was grateful. After Sarah, my first child, was born, I often walked to Pound Hill with her in the buggy (stroller) to visit Thea and Sophie. It was a quiet and pleasant time. We walked along a footpath through fields of grass and wildflowers, through gnarled trees, and a bridge over a stream.

I remember very little of the political ramifications of the times, but I remember our food budget dropped severely, and any extra spending dropped to zero. Train fares had doubled since we moved, yet the stipend for working in London didn't increase. By 1977, we struggled to maintain a healthy balance of living and paying bills. We didn't have a fixed mortgage, so to avoid losing our home, we continued to pay the increasing interest rates until it topped out between thirteen and fifteen percent. William bought a motorcycle as a more economical way to travel to work.

Phone lines were expensive back then, and many households didn't have them installed. We wrote letters, visited families, or made calls from a phone kiosk or from a close neighbor who had a phone. In the case of an emergency, the local bobby (a policeman) would pay a visit.

It was about 4:00 p.m. I had just arrived home from visiting an elderly friend I met while working at Crawley Hospital. Sarah was two years old, and I was pregnant with my second child when there was a loud knock on the front door. A young bobby gave me his name and asked if he could come in for a few moments. I clearly remember him asking me to sit down and me replying, "I'm sorry, I have to get my daughter something to eat first. Please, tell me what has happened. Is it my husband?"

"Are you sure you won't sit down first, ma'am?"

"No, please, just tell me." Despite the turmoil I felt, my heart pounding in my chest, I was amazed at how calm I outwardly remained.

"Yes, ma'am, your husband has been in an accident, ma'am."

"Where? When?" I asked, as I lifted Sarah into the highchair and put a plate of sandwiches on the tray.

"It happened this morning, ma'am, on his motorbike."

"Drink, please, Mummy."

"I'll get you a drink in a minute, dear. Let me finish talking to the policeman first, please."

"Is he all right?"

"That's all I know, ma'am. You'll have to call the hospital to find out more."

"OK! Thank you. I've got to get back to my daughter now, sir."

"I'll say good day to you, ma'am. You sure you'll be OK?"

"Yes, I'm fine, thank you," I said, shutting the door and letting out a breath for what felt like the first time in a long while.

I hurried to feed Sarah, gave her a quick wash, and changed her clothes before hurrying over to my in-laws. I had neither a phone nor a driver's license. I walked the two miles to their house, and then we drove up to London to find out how serious the accident was. Fortunately, it wasn't bad, but William had to stay in the hospital for a few days. Following this incident, I insisted that we have a phone installed, although we only used it for emergencies because of the cost of calling.

My First Two Children

My first child, Sarah, was born in May 1975. Although I had an easy pregnancy, I didn't enjoy those nine months. Because of the recession, we had no extra money for maternity clothes; I lived in a long, warm nightdress when I wasn't at work. I was thankful that I only gained a little weight. Just before the birth, on a hospital visit, a pregnant lady inquired if I was two to three months along!

Women stayed in the maternity ward for ten days after birth back then. Babies stayed in a nursery, except for feeding time, which was regulated by the nurses on a four-hour schedule, from 6:00 a.m., with no deviations. The nurses woke the babies up and brought them into our ward for the last feeding of the day at ten. The babies stayed in the nursery for the late feed to allow new mothers to sleep through the night. I refused to breastfeed because of an incident when I was fourteen. My mother handed me Sophie, who tried to latch onto me. I was horrified and unable to overcome feeling like a cow.

I believed if I breastfed my baby, I'd transfer my trauma to my child, and the baby would feel my abhorrence. I bottle-fed using Ostermilk* baby formula. Hospital visitors, including the fathers, were not allowed to hold the babies, but I managed to sneak my baby out of the nursery when Sarah was eight days old and let William cuddle her.

I remember William returning to the hospital later in the day after the birth with a stuffed dog—it was the size of an adult human—and a bottle of Ballantine's. It was the first time I had tasted whiskey. I looked at William and smiled, "Humm, so smooth. Can I have another sip, please?"

I watched from a window in the maternity ward when William left the hospital. He strapped the toy dog to the passenger seat on his motorbike, its legs hung over the side and William put the spare helmet on its head. He told me later, he visited his parents, his sister, and her husband, John. Christopher, his brother, was abroad visiting his grandparents in Australia. Afterwards, he went around Crawley, celebrating the birth of his daughter and sharing his bottle of Ballantine's.

Thani, our cat, definitely considered himself the boss of the household. When I first brought Sarah home, Thani took one look at the baby and turned his back on William and me for a few weeks, refusing to bring us 'gifts' from the garden, for which I was thankful, but he also refused to curl up on the settee with me in the evening if the baby was up. When we got a second kitten, Emma, to keep her company, Thani

*Ostermilk was a popular brand of baby formula. Developed in the 1960s it was discontinued in 1985 because of a salmonella outbreak.

let Emma know who was the boss. She chased the poor thing all around the room and up the open weave lace curtains until Emma submitted to being the inferior cat. Thani refused to wash himself from then on; it was Emma's job for the rest of their lives together.

Two years later, while pregnant with my second child, I had a job selling Avon cosmetics. I rode door-to-door on my bicycle with Sarah in the carrier Don had made for Sophie when she was an infant. Although I wasn't comfortable talking to strangers, the women I met loved to talk about babies. They loved predicting the sex of my expected baby, which they all said would be a boy. The women usually had biscuits or candy to give my daughter and a cup of tea for me. It was a great icebreaker. I had a lot of fun, made money, and won awards and gifts.

I was seven months pregnant when the country celebrated the Queen's Silver Jubilee in June 1977. Our estate committee chose me to represent the Queen in the pageant as I was the only pregnant lady in our complex—the officials said it made their job easier. I rode around on the back of a trailer, waving at the crowds of neighbours. It was fun. The best part was Sarah, who wore a Tinkerbell outfit, which her dad cut out and I stitched together. She won a Koala bear and a plastic train for the best costume.

Fourteen days after my second baby was due, I began the same irregular contractions I had with Sarah, but I was eager to give birth and get rid of the weight I carried around. William called his mother to come and stay with Sarah. After I collected my bag, already packed for two weeks, I whispered to my belly, "Listen, baby, it's time. You've had fourteen extra days lounging around in the dark warmth. It's time to come out and see the world."

"The midwife will meet us at the hospital," William said when he returned from calling his mother. "I've got the car running. Mum will be here in a moment."

"Well, baby, we'll see if those ladies were right. You'd better be a boy. We've not come up with a girl's name."

Everything was different this time; I only had a midwife and my husband in the room, the lights were low, and there was soft music. I was given gas for this birth because of my reactions the first time to pethidine, an opioid pain relief drug. Barely dilated, I insisted I was ready to push. The midwife explained she would break my waters so things would happen quickly. I felt a surge of pain shoot through me, and hot liquid flowed out on the sheets. Five minutes later, the baby was born. Still attached to the placenta, the midwife laid the baby skin to skin on my chest. He was a peaches and cream baby, unlike my daughter, who had struggled to be born because I hadn't known I was ready to push. I was happy that my husband could hold the baby so soon after birth. Birthing had changed in the short time since my daughter was born. It was so much better. I only stayed in the hospital for twenty-four hours and had a private room.

When Sarah came in with her father and grandparents, she wasn't interested in chocolate, cookies, candy, or me. She ran through the ward shouting,

"Where's my baby?" making the nurses and other mothers laugh. The next day, when the ambulance brought me home, we almost lost Sarah in her excitement to see the baby. She escaped out of the back gate when the dustmen (trash collectors) arrived, just as William came out of the front door to meet me.

"My baby, not yours," she said to me.

My son, Richard, was a sweet, tranquil baby, happy to lie and view the world around him. His devoted sister met his simple needs. In the spring of 1978, when we went to the U-pick farm for strawberries, he was sitting up but not crawling. Dressed in blue and white checked pants and a smocked top, I sat him in the middle of a strawberry row while we filled our buckets.

"Look, Mummy, he loves them," Sarah declared as she ran back and forth, inserting strawberries into his ever-open mouth.

"All we need is the sugar and cream," William's mother said laughingly.

I reckoned that by the time we left that field, Richard had consumed at least a pound of strawberries without uttering a word. He slept well later that afternoon and wasn't sick.

Travelling by Train

Sometime in 1976, I went for a weekend visit to see Mummy, Daddy, and Lorna in Slapton Sands, Devon, without William or Sarah.

I boarded a train in Three Bridges, went to Victoria Station, then the underground to Paddington, and a train from there to Southwest England. I had a few hours to relax before I reached Paignton Station, where I would transfer to an older, smaller, smoke-belching train. I read my book until we passed Reading and were out of the big city. Then I put my book down, leaned back on the seat, and stared through the grimy window, listening to the mesmerising clickity-clack of the wheels on the tracks. Passing through numerous small villages, I enjoyed looking into the gardens of the row houses, rumpled with living, backed up against the railroad line. I also saw many church steeples dotted throughout the towns and countryside and invented stories of the people in those places.

I recall school children in blue and red checkered uniforms standing in the overcast steel-gray weather, waving at the train while waiting at the barriers for it to pass. The children were probably on their way home for lunch. I waved back, taking delight in seeing their rosy faces light up for a second before they were gone.

I reminisced back to when I was fifteen, still at school, lonely, uprooted from the security of my home in the sun. I was timid and reserved, too shy to wave to strangers, even when passing on a train.

I also remembered another weekend about the same period. I'd recently become a Girl Guide and was excited to show Lorna and Francis my uniform and tell them about all the badges I would take. I felt smart and older in my crisp blouse, and new style dark straight skirt, and an air hostess look-a-like hat. I was happy, smiling as I watched the towns and countryside slip by the window when a stranger sat in the seat next to me.

He leaned in close, breathing into my ear, and placed his hand on my leg, whispering, "What's your name, dearie? Where are you going?"

I felt trapped with no other passengers in the carriage; his hand moved under my skirt. He asked me to get off the train with him. "Why?" I asked as I moved my leg away from him, crossed it over my other leg, and pulled my bag onto my lap. "This isn't my stop. If I got off here, it would be silly. I'd only have to get back onto the next train." The man shook his head, got up, and walked away. I wondered if he had thought me stupid. I believed my naivety saved me.

Now, I was older and more relaxed. I had been married a couple of years, had a child, and was eager to have a few days unencumbered by my husband or child. I turned my thoughts to window shopping in Dartmouth, walking along the boulevard, and watching the ships and yachts moored on the River Dart.

I hoped Lorna would be content to do her market shopping without me. Unlike Anne, she was very predictable. I knew what Lorna would purchase: chicken pate, pork pies with shiny hot-water pastry, bunches of parsley, fresh tomatoes and carrots, and local potatoes from the market. Afterwards, she'd insist that we walk up the hill to the butcher together, to buy beef, chicken, or a leg of lamb for Sunday dinner, sausages, and perhaps bacon and fresh farm eggs for the rest of the week. Lorna considered herself a gourmet cook. I loved good food, but to me, Lorna ruined all her vegetables by adding homemade white and parsley sauces. Like Mummy, I preferred the taste of unadulterated carrots, peas, spinach, or other vegetables.

Needing to stretch my body after sitting on the train for a few hours, I got up to go to the WC. Inside the closed cubicle, the smell of old urine mixed with disinfectant and the brackish smell of stale water was overpowering. The sign over the sink told passengers not to drink the water. I felt nauseated. Who would want to drink that water? I didn't even want to wash my hands in it.

On my way back to my seat, I stood at the open window in the corridor between the carriages. I loved the feel of the powerful rush and muscle of the wind, although I knew it would twist my lightweight hair into knots, and I'd have to struggle to comb out the tangles before I reached Paignton. Still, I put my head out as far as I dared, remembering a story I had heard many years ago of two trains passing in opposite directions and slicing the head off the person's shoulders. I remembered my teenage mind thinking it would be so disgusting for someone else walking through the carriages to see a headless body standing at the window and wondered how I would have behaved if I had seen it.

Back in my seat, I ate my egg sandwiches and apple and drank my tea from the flask. It didn't taste good. I had waited too long, and the milk had soured slightly because of the heat on the train. By the time I finished, we were pulling into Paignton.

"All change, all change, please. The Kingswear train is waiting on platform three. Remain on this platform for the next train to Ivybridge and Plymouth. All change please, all change."

I only had a few minutes to get off the train, hurry down the stairs, and up to platforms three and four. I boarded one of the few remaining old steam trains. Each carriage had a corridor with five or six doors opening into compartments, each accommodating twelve people. Above each set of six seats were the luggage racks. I smiled, remembering the rare train trips when I was young, new to England, and my new-found siblings. We would run through the train until we found a compartment without people, climb up into the luggage racks, and lie there for a few minutes, pretending we were hidden under a blanket, hiding from a villain.

Lurching and unsteady, I walked along the corridor as the train swayed and jolted slowly along the coastline. I was looking for a compartment nearer the front of the train that had the least stale, musty smell of frequent travellers. There were no restrictions on smokers back then. I slid open doors, sniffed and if the air was unsuitable, closed them again. I walked to the next compartment and repeated the process. When I saw another person coming along the corridor towards me, I paused and looked out of the grimy window as if interested in the moving scenery. Finally, I found the right compartment. I went in, closed the door, threw my duffle bag, and myself facedown onto the seat. I was alone at last; I drew in a deep breath, allowing my fantasies to wander as at no other time in my day. I closed my eyes and began to revel in an imagined Agatha Christie drama—the train was pristine, full of wealthy people chugging along through beautiful scenery. A murder had been committed, and I would solve it.

Through my dreaming, I heard the door open again, and from the corner of my eye, I saw a trousered leg moving into the compartment and heard the swish and slide of the door closing.

"Is this seat taken?"

"No, it isn't." What else could I say?

I sat up quickly, resenting this stranger breaking into my space, opened my eyes, and brought myself back into the present. I saw a middle-aged man in a slightly shiny as if ironed one time too many, black suit, a black briefcase, black shoes, and an ugly blue and gold tie. I turned away, hoping he would change his mind and try a different carriage. But he sat down opposite me and started a conversation.

"How far are you going?"

"Dartmouth," I replied without lifting my eyes. I was thinking, "Oh God, here we go again."

"Nice place," he said as if the conversation was getting comfortable.

"Yes," I replied and looked away.

"Do you live there?"

"No!" I wished he'd stop talking. However, he persisted, and I thought it rude not to answer when spoken to.

"I thought you looked lonely and might like some company."

"No, Thank you, I am fine on my own," I answered, looking him directly in the eyes without smiling.

I could feel and smell the sweat building up under my arms. I was nervous, I got up, undecided about what to do next. The man stood up, and before I could move, he pinned me against the window, his mouth on mine.

I could hear my heart pounding in my ears, but I willed myself to remain calm. I let my mind go blank, not seeing or hearing but knowing I could look directly into the man's face and remain impassive. He let go of me.

I breathed out carefully, held in a shudder, and heard my voice say sarcastically,

"Did you enjoy that?"

The next few seconds moved as if in a time warp. The man turned, picked up his briefcase from the seat, slid open the door, and retreated down the corridor, his footsteps creating an unrhythmical echo against the clickity-clack of the train.

Visibly shaking, I sat down. I had played a role, thankfully, to my advantage. I took a deep breath, releasing the tension in my body. As I did, a gurgle of laughter slipped through my lips. I heard Mummy's voice, "It is better to laugh than to cry."

I picked up my things and spent the rest of my journey in the space between the two carriages with the window open. I was happy to stand looking out over the sea, watching the children on the beach, and inhaling the briny, salty smell of the low tide, until a whistle blast and a force of air expelled as the train roared through a tunnel, caught me by surprise, making me jump back in fright.

"Did you have a good journey?" Lorna asked when she greeted me at the ferry. "You've got some colour in your cheeks. You must have been standing near an open window, your hair is a mess."

Stoicism was a word I had learnt well since I was a small child. Only I was responsible for any outcome in my life. I would tell no one of this incident, not even my husband—it would be better not to be disappointed by his lack of understanding and sympathy.

Life Changing Events

Trauma happens to all of us, and we hopefully learn to be resilient. But past events can live silent and dark in our minds, affecting our capacity to love unconditionally.

Sudden, intense emotions can erupt, leaving us overwhelmed and out of control. I was over forty years old before I knew I suffered from clinical and postnatal depression. I functioned as a wife and mother by putting one foot in front of the other and kept going. I felt like I was drowning, the water just below my eyes, before I started my Avon round.

1978 was a particularly hard year. Seven months before Richard was born, Don, my stepfather, died suddenly. It was a traumatic time for the whole family, especially Sophie. After a terrible drive home from visiting her grandparents and Lorna in Devon, Sophie had rushed over to Mrs. Ridgeway, sobbing that she hated her father and wished him dead. Jim, her brother, knocked on the door before she had time to finish a cup of tea. Don had died.

Don suffered from paranoia, detachment from reality, extreme panic attacks, and chest pains since I was living with the family. His doctors considered him a hypochondriac but never considered diagnosing him with a severe mental breakdown after an incident with an Army cadet where he received two black eyes, which put him in bed, believing he would be dead in three days. His fear, pain, hallucinations, and heart issues were the eventual cause of his death. Sophie was under fourteen years old.

When Don died, Thea was left financially destitute. He'd never divorced his first wife. On his tax forms each year, he declared Thea, the mother of his child, as a housekeeper, and their bank account was in his name only. Don's legal wife got everything, from death benefits to life insurance. There was no one to help Thea financially, and her vulnerability attracted a group of evangelists, who persuaded her to join them, much to my horror.

I remember it as a bewildering and stressful time. I was angry and sad, with a feeling of being out of control. I couldn't help anyone; William and I had no extra money, and I feared for Sophie, she was young and still at school. At home, I often felt I had failed in my daily life, despite what I see now as success, making do on very little. I also dreamt constantly of dying or losing my children.

I tried to help William financially with the continued increase in the cost of living: I pushed myself to add more people to my Avon round. I cut back on the shopping, checked prices in the stores before I bought groceries, and kept nutritious food on the table. My monthly household allowance was £100. Utilities were a minimum of £30 each. But, if I was careful, once I paid the monthly bills and bought food, we might have £1 over at the end of the month, which I'd saved in case of emergencies.

I wanted William to understand and appreciate all I was doing to help. I wanted to be held and told everything would work out, but he had his own worries and traumas: The long days of travelling to work, the constant vigilant of riding a bike through London, and the stress of his job.

With two children to manage, I put them to bed early before their tired grizzles (crying) wore me down, and I lost my temper. It was better for me, but William only saw his children at weekends. I wanted to be close. He wanted space. One day, he yelled at me, "You're a nymphomaniac," and slapped me away from him. I wanted companionship. He heard sex. I kept the fear and loneliness inside most of the time, but peace was hard to come by, and there was often an eruption of anger between us.

Looking back, I believe some of my anger against men began around this time. One afternoon, before my second child was born, I had a visit by two men from the NSPCC (The National Society for the Prevention of Cruelty to Children.) A neighbour, they said, had called. "You leave your child alone and go out," they said.

"Yes," I replied. "It is easier to do my Avon round while she is asleep. I can go and come back before she wakes up."

Sarah loved her bedroom. She would often wake from her two-hour nap in the afternoons and play happily for another hour. William built a net frame that fitted into the door of her bedroom, which allowed air into the room while preventing her from exiting and falling down the stairs. I knew Sarah would be safe until I returned.

It may have been wrong according to the law, but from my perspective, my daughter and I got to do the things that made us happy without demands from each other. The occasional going out gave me breathing space and kept me sane.

Sarah was awake and playing with a Tupperware Shapes Ball while the men were in the house. They kept exclaiming how bright and alert she was and how clear her speech was. "She is so intelligent." They kept exclaiming.

"Thank you," I said smiling, "I spend a lot of time talking with her."

I was surprised and angry with their next statement, "We could break down your front door and come in another time."

My pulse racing, I replied in quiet fury, "You, a stranger to my child, would break down my front door and take my terrified child from her bed. Are you mad? Is that, in your opinion, a better, safer, healthier experience for a child? To take her screaming out of her bed and home? I don't think so. Please go away, leave us alone."

"We will come back when your husband is home," they said and left.

By the time William came home, I was a nervous wreck. I couldn't do anything except sit and stare at Sarah playing. When the men returned, William told them that it was his fault. He said he didn't spend much time with me and the child, as he studied every evening. He promised that he would change. The course was nearly over, and he would have more time for family. The men left satisfied with William's guarantee. "Your wife will be happier if you spend more time with her."

It did work for a while. We spent more time talking, and William broached the idea of giving up his work at the hospital—he wanted to be an artist. But when he told his mother, she was so upset about him giving up his career that I knew he never would.

By the summer of that year, our lives were about to change significantly. Sarah was three, and Richard was almost a year old. I was beginning to worry because William was late coming home one Friday evening. But when he walked through the door, and before I could express my relief, he announced, "I talked to a lady at the estate agents at Three Bridges—she's coming round tomorrow to look at our house and put it on the market!"

I was speechless. With the birth of my second child, life for me was happier. I had friends and purpose. I enjoyed my nights working in a nursing home with the elderly people who became my friends. The Avon round was enjoyable and gave me an income and a social outlet—those clients became good friends.

Despite the high-density housing of the area where we lived, our house was pretty inside and now had a small garden on either side of the front door—an upright yew tree softened one wall, and a hedge on the other side separated us from the neighbours. The kitchen window facing the entrance had pretty blue and white gingham curtains with a wide stiffened frill on the edge.

The first prospective buyer through our door bought it for £25,000. Even though we had not begun to look for a place in London or tell our friends and family, William agreed to move out in three weeks without giving me any choice in the decision.

1978–1982
Prah Road
London

Relocating

Our house on Oulton Walk sold, and our move-out date became imminent, but we didn't have a place to live. I concentrated all my energy on caring for the children, working my Avon round, and packing our home and belongings. While at work, William drew concentric circles starting from Central London to find and view available three-bedroom houses in the area until the prices met his budget.

Although William's parents had two spare bedrooms, they refused to provide us with temporary housing. Friends of mine, Lynda and George, and godparents to my son suggested we move into the room where her mother had lived in her last years. We must have stored our furniture somewhere, and then the four of us, two cats, a double and single mattress, a cot, a bunch of boxes, and all our clothes, moved into a room sixteen by eighteen feet, plus a built-in wardrobe and a bay window. It was a tight fit. The children had always had their own rooms. I felt it was easy for William as he left the house before six in the morning and didn't return until after eight once the children were asleep.

I was apprehensive about moving to London, and telling my friends and family was difficult. All I could say was, "William wants to be nearer his work." My best friend at the time was so hurt that she never spoke to me again. She believed I had known about the move before I told her. The hardest people to tell were the women from the Avon round. For a while, I couldn't. I continued to travel back to Crawley with the children every week for two months after we finally moved to visit my clients and deliver their Avon before I could let go of these special, loving people.

With the difficulty of traveling with two young children or getting a babysitter and the prohibitive cost of fares to London, I didn't view any of the houses William looked at after work until we had been with Lynda and George for a week. William found a place he considered the best deal, we left the children with my in-laws and went to London to see the house on the Holloway Road.

From the outside, the house looked like all the rest on the street—stucco over brick, with Victorian/Gothic moldings around the windows and doors. But inside, the rooms were small and dirty. The kitchen was an illegal lean-to built over a manhole (sewage access). The upstairs room had a drop-down ladder and was bolted and padlocked by the young renter who lived there—we couldn't view the room. To top it off, there was no garden or green space anywhere. We politely said goodbye and left.

I was furious when William said, "Well, what do you think?"

Commonsense and the obvious problems made me yell at him, "Are you crazy!" "That was an illegal extension. I'm not cooking in a kitchen with a sewage drain in it. I will NOT move into that house with our two children."

"Well, we have to find a house today."

I remained quiet. What else could I say? He was

my husband. We drove around until we came to an area called Finsbury Park. Suddenly, William stopped the car. "I see an estate agent across the road," "You wait here, and I'll go and see if there is anything for sale in this area."

I thought it was a slightly nicer-looking area. I saw a lovely green park beyond beautifully wrought iron gates. At least, I thought, there would be somewhere to bring the children to play. What I didn't realise was that the men standing around the gate were the local drunks and addicts.

William came back excited, saying, "There's a house just around the corner on Prah Road for sale. Let's go take a look. We are running out of time. I refuse to go back to Crawley without finding another place." Using his much-thumbed *London A-Z* (a book of all the streets in London), he drove down Blackstock Road, turned onto Rock Street, and then onto Prah Road. We passed what I thought was a local school, but I found out later it was a secretarial college, a beautiful red-orange Victorian brick building.

The house we were looking for was located at the convergence of three roads. It was unoccupied, "That means a quick sale," William said. We looked through the large bay window but couldn't see much. I was unimpressed but didn't feel I could say anything.

The house was a Victorian, three-storied terraced row house built in the 1880s with shared side walls. The right side joined at an angle greater than ninety degrees to number 1 Romilly Road. William called the estate agent the next morning and arranged to view the house on Monday before he went to work. He made an offer and then called our mortgage company's home inspector.

The inspection showed structural damage. The front wall and bay window would require attention before the bank would loan any money. Other repairs were also necessary, but the wall was the major problem. I suggested writing directly to the seller—by-passing the estate agent. But William ignored me and only told the estate agent why we wanted a price reduction.

Two weeks later, we still had not heard from the estate agent. At this point, I decided to take matters into my own hands. I wrote to the seller, Mr. Rashid, who lived in Derbyshire. Forty-eight hours later, I received a call from Mr Rashid from a pay phone—I heard the coins drop into the box so fast that the sound burred every second word he spoke. I explained as fast as I could about the cost of the work required to make the house safe. I deliberately doubled the highest bid we had received to £3000, and Mr. Rashid agreed to drop the price by half. I was elated and called William at work, "Darling, I got £1500 off the selling price."

"Did we get a letter from the estate agent?" William asked.

"No, I wrote directly to the owner. He called me today. It was so funny I could hear the money falling in the box faster than we were speaking."

"Why did you do that?"

"I was tired of nothing happening. You're not the one here all day with the children. Lynda's never had children, and she has all her precious things everywhere.

You come home, and they are bathed and ready for bed."

"OK!" William sighed, "Let's not get into that! What did the owner say?"

"I asked for £3000 in the letter, and he agreed to meet us halfway, so we got the £1500 we needed. Isn't that great?"

"You should have called me and let me handle it. It wasn't your place to do that. I could have got more!"

"I did suggest you write to the owner, but you didn't, so I did. It is done, and now we can move."

The estate agent wasn't happy with what I had done either, but the house was now ours. William hired a company to rip up the linoleum on the ground floor, stairs, bathroom, and bedrooms on the first floor and spray the bare wood with a quick penetrating and drying solution to kill the dry rot and woodworm infestation. The company told him the fumes would not be harmful after twenty-four hours.

London at Last

When we eventually moved, I felt very little excitement. I had made the sale happen and received no gratitude. I was worried about the children, especially Sarah, leaving her friends and school behind and moving to a place where we knew no one. I was stressed from living in one small bedroom for so long and continually trying to manage two children in my friend's home who had never had children.

The Saturday we moved was a balmy mid-morning at the end of September 1978. Christopher, William's brother, had offered to help us, but on the day we were ready, he had a black belt judo competition. My in-laws were willing to look after the children for the day, but not overnight. We were on our own.

When we pulled the moving van into the driveway of our new home, William's face showed determination. Mine? I felt worried, exhausted, and trepidatious. I had never seen inside the house except through the large, sagging bay window.

I couldn't believe we were to live in this house when we walked through the front door. It looked awful, unfit for family living. The smell of the wood rot treatment brought tears to my eyes. I wondered silently how I would cope with the two children in this house, one of whom had not yet begun to walk.

We did have running cold and hot water from a gas water heater, but we didn't have any electricity. I swept the large front room floor, ready to take all our possessions except the stove, while William unlocked the truck and connected the ramp. "Well, we had better get unloaded," he said. "We've got a lot to do today, and we have to return the van by 5 p.m."

"We'll manage," I said, picking up a box and carrying it inside.

We took the stove out first, placing it on the lower, cold concrete floor of the two-tiered, dirty space accessed off the hallway, which would become our kitchen.

Tired and dusty five hours later, we locked the house, and William drove the hour and a half back to Crawley. We returned the truck before the office closed for the weekend, picked up the car, had dinner at my in-laws, and drove back to Lynda's. I put the children to bed. Then I called my younger brother, Jim, a contractor at the time, to ask him what to do about the floors. Even after I had swept them, a sticky black residue lay on the floor. He suggested tacking heavy-duty plastic onto the floor, which he promised to bring us from his construction company the following week.

We drove back to London in the morning with the children and the two cats to begin our new life, far away from family support. It was then William told me about the electrical situation. "When the man from the electricity board came to turn on the meter, there was a big bang. I felt sorry for the poor bloke. I don't know how he didn't get electrocuted. He threw the switch, and a blue flash lit up the basement! 'Can't turn that on for yer,' he said. 'Here's what I'll do for yer, I'm a family man too.'"

The electrician showed William how to bypass the meter with a single electrical cable, with a socket on the end of it. "He told me," William said, "I'll give you a month. That should give you enough time to get the ground floor wired for lights and sockets."

"Wow! That was nice of him," I said. "Isn't it illegal?"

"The man said it'll be all right, William replied. "No one would know, and he'd be back in a month and connect it properly."

Our means of electricity for the next month was a long, single, heavy-duty extension cable running from behind the meter box in the tiny basement up to the ground floor. A single socket was attached to the end of the cable, into which we plugged a kettle for tea and power tools as William needed. At night, we plugged another extension into the socket for a light, which we trailed up and down three flights of stairs and into the bathroom.

William bought a book called *How to Wire A House* and followed it carefully. He worked very hard in the evenings, after his regular job, and at weekends until he took a second job as a security guard on Friday and Saturday nights.

For the first couple of weeks, the only room clean enough for the children was the small room at the top of the house. I found that working on our new home was exciting at first, but by the end of the month, the novelty was wearing thin. I was taking care of two children, carrying them up and down the stairs, cooking, washing clothes in a bathtub, and working on the house while they were both asleep in the afternoons.

William still worked at the Royal Marsden Hospital in Chelsea as a laboratory researcher, then came home, ate, and worked on the house for two or three hours until it became too dark to see. My job was to keep the children happy and have dinner ready when William came home. At the end of the first two weeks, we had sockets on the ground floor and lights in the kitchen but nothing on the staircase or bathroom. William did incredible work, but it was still a difficult time. Resentments spilled out with William saying, "It's all right for you. You don't have to go to work—you're at home all day."

I'd snap back, "You at least have a clean, warm place to go to every day." I wanted at least to be told I was also doing a good job.

Things changed after I tripped over the trailing wires and one of the cats on the stairs with Richard in my arms. I let out words I did not know I had bottled inside me. I was surprised when William accepted my tirade without a word. We went back to working on our projects and not interfering with each other. Mildly and infrequently, we remembered to thank each other. All the walls in the house were lathe and plaster, and the cavities were full of aged soot from wood and coal fires, mouse droppings, accumulated dirt, and an occasional old newspaper. This meant constant dust and grime-filled air in the rooms, which most probably contained asbestos. Keeping the children clean was almost impossible. We were all sick with coughs and headaches, and the children got worms from the dirt.

William expected Jim to give us the roll of heavy-duty plastic for free and was extremely angry when Jim insisted on payment for the wholesale cost. The ensuing argument caused a delay of a couple of months, which affected me and the children. It stuck another wedge between my family and me, and I took the brunt of the blame. Until the floor was covered, I had to carry Richard everywhere when he wasn't asleep in his crib.

9 Prah Road

My memory of how I managed our two cats—how and when I let them out—is a mystery. I'm sure it was only for short periods in the begining—litter boxes were unheard of in those days. I must have fed them under the table in the kitchen. Emma was a roamer, and Thani, the highly strung Siamese, the alpha, was finicky and demanding. I had to be careful with doors and windows, keeping them closed most of the time as we lived on a main road.

I cleaned up the small garden at the back of the house while William was at work during the first month. It was full of rubbish, including needles, presumably thrown over from the building behind us. The garden wall between us and our neighbours on the Prah Road side was breaking down and sliding into their garden. Almost every house in the area had work being done. It was a common sight to see large skips (dumpsters) in the streets.

Most days, I would leave the children in the back upstairs bedroom, three floors up, overlooking the garden, with toys and books. I would prop open the window enough to hear the children call out, but not so much as they could lean out or get cold. I have often wondered how many times a day I ran up and down those stairs each time Sarah called out, "Mummy!"

When I wasn't cleaning up outside, I worked on the kitchen and the dining room, as we needed somewhere comfortable to eat. Our kitchen was a narrow pie-shaped space off the hallway to the right of the front door, with a two-step drop down to a stone floor. The upper part would eventually have a bar-style counter and tall stools for the children to sit on. There was a small window on the outside wall, which we never opened, but it let in great light. In the lower part, a large stone sink sat under the window, which looked out onto a mess of weeds, bricks, and old drug paraphernalia. In the corner of the room was the gas water heater with a door leading to a four-foot square space, with two more doors, one into the garden and the other into the basement, which housed the electrical meter. On the opposite wall of the kitchen were a table and a couple of cupboards. The other item in this space was a large bathtub with a wooden cover in three pieces for easy removal. Our gas stove sat between the tub and the steps.

Until the dining room was clean enough, meal times were interesting. I cooked and took the food upstairs to the back bedroom. I learnt quickly not to forget anything. For the children's lunch, their main meal of the day, I would load a tray with the two meals, often stews cooked from scratch, with lots of vegetables, potatoes, meat, and gravy. I diluted Ribena or orange squash for the children, tea for me, and pudding, usually blancmange, fruit, or jelly. I always put a wet flannel (washcloth) on the tray for cleaning up afterwards.

After lunch, I'd change Richard's nappy before putting him in his cot, then help Sarah in the bathroom on the first landing. The last thing I did before the children went to sleep was to read them a story. As they slept for at least two hours, it gave me plenty of time to do household tasks.

Once William finished the wiring on the ground floor, he installed the washing machine. A month isn't long without a washing machine. But with two small children, one still in nappies, and with the grime in the house, washing clothes was an ordeal—an all-day event. I would fill the bathtub in the kitchen with scalding water from the water heater. I started with clean whites: bed linen, children's vests (they both wore them in those days), and light-coloured shirts and blouses. I left them soaking in hot water for an hour or until I'd cleaned the floors, fed the children, and took Sarah to play school (pre-school). Once home again, Richard would take a nap, and I would wash, wring out the first load as best as I could, empty the tub, and fill it again with warm water. Then I rinsed, wrung, and piled the clothes, still dripping, into a large, heavy plastic bag inside a folding utility cart and started the next load. I kept going until it was time to pick up Sarah at lunchtime. Then I sat Richard on top of the bag of wet clothes and lugged them down to the launderette to spin in a high-speed spinner, loaded everything back into the cart, picked up Sarah, and came home. I gave the children lunch, and while they ate, I hung the washing on the line in the back garden or on a clothes horse at the front of the house. It was quite an orchestrated event. It never occurred to me to ask William to help with this task. This was considered women's work, and I did it cheerfully.

Bath time for the children was in the same tub. I

would run the water, fetch Richard and all the clean clothes, and carry them to the kitchen while Sarah ran ahead of me. I'd undress the children on the table by the stove while I checked the water temperature, then lift Richard in while Sarah climbed in. The floors were still too cold and nasty for them to stand on. After the bath, I'd dry Richard first, change him on the table, carry him upstairs, and put him in his cot. I would return downstairs for Sarah, who already pulled the plug and was ready for me to dry and dress her. Afterwards, we'd walk upstairs together, avoiding touching the walls or the banisters; there was always fine black dust everywhere and probably splinters in the wood.

One evening, we had more excitement than we bargained for. I was bathing the children, and William was outside. He stepped forward to wave to the children and disappeared immediately. At first, I thought William was playing peek-a-boo with them. When he didn't reappear, and I went outside to check—William had fallen into the open manhole. He had taken the lid off to check on a sewer blockage.

I helped haul William out by locking my arms under his armpits and pulling while he pushed with his one good leg. His other leg had a nasty cut, with exposed bone, on his shin. While William sat with his head between his knees, I called an ambulance and searched through the list from the babysitting association for a sitter. This was not how I expected to meet my neighbours, but because I did not drive, I had no choice. The husband from a family across the street was the only person available to babysit. It was a scary experience.

With no heating for the first three months of living in London, it was harder for the children and me to stay in the house during the day. As the weather became colder, we met with other families we now knew in the area and went to the toy library or someone's warm home. Many of the houses, like ours, were in different stages of demolition and restoration.

Early Renovations

William hired a small builder's company in Crawley that had previously worked for his parents. We knew and trusted them, and they were eager to take on the job if we allowed them to set up camp in one of the rooms during the week to save on travel time. Since it was a three-story house and we mainly lived on the top floor, we saw no reason not to. Although not close friends, Michael and Paul were not strangers, and this arrangement would make the work cheaper. They managed everything from tearing down walls to installing complete room fittings, carpentry, windows, plumbing, central heating, and more. There was no need for subcontractors.

They started work on the four tiny rooms above the kitchen. The space, which was common in rented old houses in London, was divided into small rooms. There was one toilet room, three wash basin rooms, and a storage section in the middle, which housed a hot water tank and airing cupboard (a cabinet made for a hot water tank, with shelves for warming clothes). With the dividing walls removed, the room would become a glorious and luxurious bathroom. I believe that this initial work took about three weeks. I dealt with any questions about practical things during the day, but William oversaw their work and ordered the materials needed. Occasionally, I included the men in our dinner so William could talk to them.

There were many incidents of hilarity and horror as the builders ripped away those walls and installed new ones. I came home one lunchtime to find the kitchen ceiling had collapsed. Debris was everywhere! I dealt with the children first as they were hungry, making a quick picnic lunch of jam sandwiches and apple slices, which they ate outside the front door. I put them down for their afternoon naps, and while they slept, I worked feverishly to get the kitchen back to normal. I cleaned the stove, the floor, and the bath, which was still our only one at the time. It wasn't until I had finished that I noticed our beautiful ten-inch round of Stilton cheese, which sat on a shelf above the stove. In England, cheese bought whole from a dairy wasn't wrapped in plastic but covered with a thick layer of moldy cheesecloth and aged in caves for ten years or more—we'd driven home from visiting Devon, through the Cheddar Gorge especially to buy the cheese. One did not keep cheese in a refrigerator. Unfortunately, we had placed the Stilton above the cupboards in the kitchen. It was now embedded with more than an inch of ceiling plaster, dust, and soot.

The builders were amazed that I didn't freak out at the mess and relieved that I saw the funny side of the problem. "It is Stilton, after all," I said. "I can scrape the ceiling off the cheese and still enjoy the rest."

One of the men said, "My wife would leave me if I expected her to live in a house in this state."

When the builders removed the old toilet, they stood back aghast— the building's integral structure was compromised. In a previous conversion, someone cut the joists at the back apex and the angled wall to make room for the toilet outflow pipe—the toilet was supported only by its S-bend.

When the new toilet was installed and working, the old windows were out, and the new ones were ready to be put in place. Before starting work, one of the men was caught using the toilet as a double-decker bus stopped outside the window. The passengers on the top deck had a front-row view into the bathroom through the large opening. Later in the day, when Michael told me the story, he said while laughing, "What was I to do? I waved, and they waved back."

This became an anecdotal story told many times to our friends. The day Michael and Paul finished and left for Crawley, Sarah, excited at having toilet paper on a roll, flushed too much down the bowl—causing a blockage! We called Michael that evening and explained the issue. He laughed good-naturedly and said, "That's OK, kids will be kids, we'll come back tomorrow and fix the problem." With the bathroom completed, there was some pleasure in living in our house.

The next job was laying down the heavy-duty plastic on the floor my brother had finally brought us. I started in the large playroom on the first floor to make it safe for the children. It took hours of painstakingly stapling along all the wall edges throughout the house.

I did all the rooms and stairs except the kitchen and the living room. It would eventually become a lovely sitting room with a bay window, but until then, it was a junk pile of tools, furniture, and unopened boxes while we were working on the house. William and I often laughed about how, in searching for different boxes, we moved things out to the edges of the room and back to the center. It would be a couple more years before it became an empty room, and we could decorate. Once the plastic was down, I moved the table and chairs into the dining room, and we ate our meals in comfort. Richard could now go on the floor to play because I cleaned the floor twice a day.

The kitchen, with its strange shape and space on two levels, was the next project. The upper part was about five by six feet and on a level with the hallway and front door. William and I worked together, ripping out the wall and a second door. William planned to put in an archway instead to give the illusion of space. We were ripping out this wall when my in-laws, who usually never went anywhere unannounced, arrived unexpectedly. I am not sure who was more surprised. The look of consternation on June's and Bill's faces made me take a quick look up at William's face and down at our clothes. We were covered with the fine gray dust of the lime-filled lathe and plaster from the wall.

"Caught in the act of working," Bill said with a chuckle.

June looked shocked and added, "We should have called first."

William emerged from the lower half of the

kitchen, where he had gone to wash his hands. "Hi, Mum, Dad, Jane will put the kettle on while I give you a tour."

"Don't bother with tea, Jane, we'll come back another time."

At that moment, Sarah came running down the stairs, "Nanny, Grandpa."

"I'll go and get Richard, I don't want him coming down the stairs on his own," I said.

By the time I came back downstairs with Richard in my arms, William was standing outside with June and Bill. They hugged the children, gave them small bags of candy, and drove away. They did not come back to visit until the house was much more presentable and able to receive visitors. I thought they were afraid of being sucked into a void!

Against the adjoining angled wall, we planned a two-level bar-style counter with two stools on each level, but first, the wall had to be scraped, sanded, and re-plastered. I decided to tackle the task myself. I scraped and sanded the wall, which created so much dust and dried my skin and hair—sometimes, I had to shower in between sanding.

Now I needed plaster. I did not understand that I was stepping on the toes of the male-dominant world when I walked into the store. I explained what I wanted to doand asked the assistant for the correct product.

The man behind the counter sold me a ten-pound bag of fine pink powder. "This will mix to a smooth, quick-drying paste," he said.

I struggled for hours with the fine plastering

powder to get the right consistency and not have it dry out before I finished. When William came home, I was very proud of my smooth wall. In the morning, it was a different story. The thin layer of plaster had dried and bowed away from the wall. I had to tear it off and start again. I could have cried with frustration.

William laughed and commiserated with me. "They sold you the wrong product, that's why. You'd better let me get it next time."

"Not this time," I said, "I'm going to give them a piece of my mind."

"Be it on your head then."

Armed with the indignation of being made a fool of, I walked into the store determined to get better service. "I may be a woman, but I am capable of doing a job right if I'm given the right tools."

The man behind the counter smirked.

"Yesterday, you sold me some plaster."

"Yes, Miss," he said. "Didn't it work for you?"

"I am not a Miss, and of course it didn't, you sold me the wrong plaster."

"Wrong! We gave you what you asked for, didn't we?"

"Not really, you sold me plaster, but it was finishing plaster, even though I explained what I wanted it for."

"It was just our little joke, Miss, no harm done," he said with a smile.

I drew myself up to stand as tall as my five foot two and a half inches would allow, expelled a lung full of air, and told him what I thought of his joke.

"Now, I'd be happy if you'd sell me the right

product so I can do the job correctly and not waste more time."

Although I didn't care if I had to pay for more materials, the shop assistant didn't charge me extra for the proper plaster, which made me happy. Because of the dust created by the sand, I experimented by using a soft wet cloth to smooth out the rough edges of the plaster. It worked like a dream. When the wall was finally finished, it looked good; it wouldn't have passed as professional, but once painted, the irregularities faded away. I felt that I was contributing to the house and became the official plasterer of small jobs in the house. But the lime used in the old lathe and plaster made my hands swell—after finishing the work in the kitchen, I had to have my wedding ring enlarged by two sizes before I could wear it again.

After three months of hard work, we gave ourselves a break and visited Mummy, Daddy, and Lorna in Devon for Christmas. We had a lovely time until we arrived home and found a couple of inches of snow inside the upstairs bedroom window. That prompted William to secure a small loan from the bank and call our builders from Crawley again. They agreed to install radiator heating throughout the house. We had a lovely bathroom, a functional kitchen with a washing machine, and warm heat throughout our home once they were finished.

We were very grateful for all the work Michael and Paul did for us, but we couldn't keep asking them to travel to London, taking them away from their families for weeks. Our house needed a lot of work, inside and out, and we had to find London builders. The brick-and-mortar on the front and the side of the house needed work—a quarter-inch crack ran the full height of the house by the entrance. Above the front bay window, the wall had noticeably dropped, most probably due to bombing during WWII. The existing window was not the original. Then, there was the ceiling at the top of the hallway; it had water damage, and the centre was bowed, likely to collapse anytime. It had to be replaced.

London Builders

The cracks in the outside walls and the leak in the roof were our next priority. We applied for a government grant, but to qualify for the £6,000 we needed, the government insisted that we carry out another £6,000 of renovations. We couldn't afford the extra costs.

William found a handyman he thought would work. I was suspicious and warned him not to pay the scruffy builder any money upfront. Unfortunately, the man persuaded him otherwise, and William paid him £300. That was the last we saw of the man until he returned to claim his ladder a week later. William had wisely chained it to our front porch pillar. The man agreed to bring his partner, and they'd start with the side wall crack and the leak in the roof. A few days later, returning with the children for lunch, I was surprised and panicked to see an ambulance and a police car on the road. The policeman said, "I'm sorry, ma'am, these two men got into a fight. We're taking one to the hospital and the other to jail."

Eventually, William found an excellent bricklayer. This man was incredible. He fixed the front wall above the bay window by removing and repointing the bricks on a few rows. The illusion was perfect. It was impossible to tell that the wall was repaired, not replaced. He did the same on the side wall, although that crack did reappear five years later when we sold the house.

The removal of the ceiling at the top of the house was messy. We had a professional team of men, recommended by a friend from the babysitting circle, do the job. There were three flights of stairs from the front door to the top ceiling, an approximately 25 foot drop. The night before the men came, I taped the heavy plastic over every door, leaving only enough room to exit from our bedrooms, the bathroom, and the kitchen. It left me only a small amount to finish when we woke up.

When the work crew arrived, I watched them tape a long funnel of plastic to the top ceiling, down the stairs, and out the front door to the driveway before I left with the children for a day at the zoo. When I returned with the children in the early afternoon, the ceiling was down, and a hundred years of coal dust, plaster debris, dead birds, and mice lay outside the front door. The workers had installed a new plasterboard ceiling. Despite the incredible care to keep the debris within the funnel, dust was still everywhere.

While the children watched television, I swept

the stairs and the hall, then fed the children and put them in the bath. While they bathed, I removed the plastic from their bedroom doors and washed the floors and the landings. Once the children had gone to bed, I started cleaning at the top of the house, with our bedroom and then all the stairs to the ground floor. It was a Friday, and William wouldn't be home until the following day, so I didn't have to worry about dinner for him. It was midnight by the time I finished. By then, I was almost as black as the coal dust from the attic. I took a bath and then a shower to get clean. For the next two days, my throat felt blocked. Each time I blew my nose, the tissues were black. I'd breathed in a lot of black dirt and soot.

The leak in the roof remained a mystery. Although we had workers come, patch it, and pour bitumen, a sticky, black, highly viscous liquid, called asphalt in the United States into all visible holes and cracks, every time it rained, water found its way into our bathroom light. When we were selling the house, we prayed the sun would shine!

Dislodged

After Richard was born, my doctor suggested an IUD when I didn't want to go back on the birth control pill. She said the most effective one was the Copper Seven. It became dislodged with the moving, packing, and heavy lifting of our belongings when we sold our house and moved to London. I took a long time to find a doctor—I did go to a couple of clinics in our area, but the doctors I saw said, "It isn't our responsibility." On the days I went back to Crawley on the train—taking the children with me—for my Avon round —I went to see my old doctor. She said it wasn't her responsibility either.

With the urgent need to create a safe, clean environment for my children, I stopped trying to find a doctor and put up with the discomfort for another year. By 1979, I was depressed and anemic. Finally, William insisted I see a doctor. I did, but he only gave me some pills. After I took one dose, I slept all day. I didn't pick up my children from play school or toddler group. I didn't hear the phone ring, nor the teachers when they knocked at my front door. I threw the rest of the pills away and went back to the doctor. "You'll have to go into the hospital for a D&C (dilation and curettage) to remove the IUD. I suggest that you have a hormone injection, Depo-Provera* for birth control because it is easier to get pregnant following a D&C."

The Archway Hospital was old. It was built as an infirmary in 1879. After I was admitted, a nurse handed me a razor and said, "Take this to the bathroom at the end of the hall. You'll need to shave down below, then wash yourself."

The bathroom was dirty— paint peeling off the walls and a hot but rusty radiator, on which I didn't dare put my clothes. I sat on the edge of a heavy enamelled bathtub as there was no chair in the room. While balancing on the edge of the bath and trying to shave

*Depo-Provera was commonly given in the UK and lasted for approximately thirteen weeks, but there was a lot of controversy about the hormone injection.

the hair between my legs, I saw a rat creeping around the opposite wall. I wanted to scream, but I only drew my feet up off the floor and shuddered. I felt unclean. I was worried and scared about the procedure. William was at work as it wasn't considered appropriate for husbands to be with their wives for female procedures.

While waiting for the doctor, I questioned the nurse about the hormone injection. I was shocked into silence when the nurse told me to "shut up and to roll over." Everything was fine for the first month after the procedure, but eventually, the blood spotting returned along with the depression. Two months later, I found out that the hormone injection had stopped working—I was pregnant for the third time. The nice part was that my body returned to normal. I no longer felt hopeless—I had something to live for.

William was quiet when I told him I was pregnant. Then he said, "I'm going to get a vasectomy. If we split in the future, I don't want any more children." I was shocked by his words. William went to a private clinic for his procedure because, with the National Health, it would take too long to get an appointment, plus they would insist on counselling first. If I had been paying attention to our emotional well-being, I would have known something was seriously wrong with our relationship.

I had not enjoyed pregnancy with my first two children. This time felt different. It helped alleviate the trauma of Lorna's phone call on January 3rd, 1980, "Daddy's gone."

"How? When? Why wasn't I told he was sick?" I said.

"It was sudden, Janie. I didn't want to upset you when he went into hospital on the first."

"I could have caught the train immediately," I replied, my voice choked in tears.

Then Lorna said, "He called out your name at the end."

I was devastated. No one had given me the choice to be by his side. Or to be at his funeral. I felt utterly bereft.

Extra Money

William worked full-time at the Royal Marsden Hospital. He was usually gone from eight in the morning to six in the evening, and then he came home and worked on the house. His salary went toward the mortgage, the bills, and house-keeping, which wasn't a large amount, adding the loan for the wall repairs left little over for anything else. I was desperate to have the house finished. I disliked the children playing in the dusty, smelly house. I knew it took money and work, and I wanted to do my part to bring in extra money for plastering and wallpapering.

The nearest convenient job was cleaning the floors at the secretarial college directly behind us. I was required to work for an hour and a half twice a day. The mornings were simple; I would leave at five and be home before the children were awake or William had left for work. The afternoons were difficult; William wouldn't be home before six, and I had to be there at four to sweep the floors before evening classes started at six. I was always stressed leaving the children alone at such a young age. But I didn't know what else to do. I often skimped on the work to get home quickly.

I left them in the playroom, explaining to Sarah that I would be gone for a short while and that they must play nicely and not leave the room until I returned. I quit the job when I came home to find Sarah, only four years old at the time, had changed her brother's poopy nappy, washed him, put on a clean one, and rinsed out the dirty one. She was thrilled by her ability to take care of her brother, but I was devastated—Sarah was too young to do a mother's work.

After that, William found a job working weekend nights as a security guard. On Fridays, he left for his regular work at 8:00 a.m. and went directly to his security job, not returning until around 9:00 a.m. on Saturday. He would sleep most of the day while I either kept the children quiet or went out for the day. He would leave again after dinner, usually by six or seven in the evening, and come back on Sunday morning. He continued this extra work until we moved again.

I had spent many evenings on my own in the early years of our marriage while William did his Open University correspondence course. Now, it was different. Once the children were in bed at six thirty, the evenings were my own. I bought a Swiss Elna sewing machine for £100; it weighed seven and a half pounds and was simple to use. It had all the magical stitches for machine appliqué. I made patchwork quilts for our beds, as gifts, and to sell. I also made appliqué jackets in satin for adults and in cotton for children and babies. I highlighted the appliqué of the jackets with embroidery. When finished, I sold them to friends or took them to local fairs and bazaars.

Ann, my friend from the playgroup, and I went to clothing factories in our area and collected an assortment of scrap fabric left outside the doors, free for anyone to take. Sometimes, there would be large bundles. Also, while shopping or visiting parks with the children, I'd search through the skips (dumpsters) placed outside old houses under renovation or being converted into flats. In them, I found many discarded pieces of antique furniture. I took them home, stripped the wood, finished, polished, and learned how to re-cane the chair seats. I still have many of those chairs in my home today.

While pregnant for the third time, I became a registered childminder. The pay was good, and I could stay home with my children. However, the first child was a disaster—she was only nine months old and screamed all day. The next child, Blaise, a cute little French boy of five months, was quiet and came to us five days a week, from 8:00 a.m. until 5:30 p.m., until he was old enough to go playschool. There were many other little children who I took care of, including a set of twin boys. Sometimes, I shopped with at least four children in buggies—I tied two double buggies together, and Sarah walked beside me. The difficulty was we straddled the pavements (sidewalks). There were so many people on the streets, but most were kind.

Driving

In the autumn of 1979, a year after we moved to London, I decided to learn to drive. I wanted more independence. I wanted to go places with the children during the weekends and holidays. I'd heard that the British School of Motoring (BSM) was the best place to learn, and there was a school on the Blackstock Road. I inquired one day and booked my first lessons. William wasn't keen for me to learn, so I asked his brother to talk to him when he visited one weekend. I was dismayed by Christopher's reply: "A woman's place is in the home. You don't need to learn to drive!"

I went to my lessons anyway. I was determined to learn to drive, although I nearly cancelled once. I came home and found Sarah had given Richard a haircut with my dressmaking scissors. I was horrified to find shallow blood-stained grooves on the top of his head and no fringe left. "Where were you?" I shouted at William in frustration, "I've only been gone just over an hour."

"I thought they'd be OK, on their own. I was working on my glass etching. It would not have happened if you'd been here, would it?"

"You couldn't keep a check on two children for an hour?" I said as I stomped away in tears.

I was seven months pregnant with my third child when I took my first driving test. The tester looked at me as he stepped into the car with his papers and said, "Pregnant women shouldn't drive." Even though I was nervous, I passed all the questions, and then we went for the drive. We started along a leafy road with parked cars on either side and children coming out of school. "When I slap the windscreen with my pad, you are to come to a complete stop," the examiner said.

In England, an emergency stop on the test must be made while travelling at the regular speed of thirty miles an hour. To avoid stalling the car, I had to depress the clutch, apply the brakes, and stop in the split second his pad hit the windscreen. I performed the maneuover perfectly but was so unhinged by the tester's attitude that, following my parallel parking and three-point turn, I turned left instead of right as instructed, and he failed me.

I took my next test nine months later, in June of 1981, with a different tester. I passed with flying colours. I started driving the children to school and taking my turn carpooling, sometimes with six children and a baby piled into the back of the car. To complete my learning experience, I planned a road trip during the school holidays with the children aged five-and-a-half, three, and nine months. I had William put seatbelts in the back seats for the children before I left—I found they were easier to manage strapped in.

I loaded the glove compartment with the *London A-Z*, and maps of the South West. The first hour of driving through London was daunting—I white-knuckled it until I reached the seventy-mile strip of motorway to Crawley, our first stop. William's parents, his siblings, aunts and uncles, his cousins, and their children all lived in Crawley. We were there in time for the street parties celebrating the royal wedding of Prince Charles and Diana. The children had a wonderful time with their cousins, some of whom they hadn't seen since we left Crawley. We, of course, visited Lynda and George and had tea in the garden. None of my family were in Crawley. Thea and Sophie had moved to Newcastle, and Jim and Sonia, his wife, were on holiday. But we did go to Oulton Walk, where we'd lived when Sarah and Richard were born.

Leaving Crawley, I headed towards the coast. The roads were easier and wider, and I gripped the steering wheel a little less. Our next destination was Tricketts Cross and Bournemouth. I was excited to see Tina. It was a long time since we'd seen each other, and she hadn't met David. There was one funny incident. We were in Tina's car, the three children sitting in the back, David screaming because he was tired. I took his dummy (pacifier), leaned back from the front seat, and popped it into his mouth. The silence was gratifying. Tina huffed a long breath out and said, "I see your point, dummies do have a purpose."

After leaving Tina, I continued along the coast through Bridport, where I was born. Avoiding Chard Hill, where Gerry, Anne's husband, died, I took the road to Exeter and then through the seaside towns to the old Library in Slapton Sands, where Mummy lived with Lorna. While staying there, we went into Dartmouth with Lorna, who still made and sold her liver patè to the local stores. We went to the beach, picked wild strawberries along the country lanes, and went to Plymouth and Dartmoor.

We had been gone for almost two weeks—it was time to head home. I took the motorway (freeway) through Yeovil and Winchester, where we stayed at the youth hostel. Once I passed through Reading, I knew we were back in London. The roads were crammed with traffic, lights, and people. I had covered over seven hundred miles through cities, narrow country roads, and motorways. I loved my feeling of independence!

Fun Times

When we moved into Prah Road in the autumn of 1978, I found travelling across London with my two small children scary. The first time, I stood at the top of the escalator in a quandary, unable to take the first step. I had Richard, a one-year-old, in his buggy and Sarah standing close to me. I was worried about falling, tipping Richard from his seat, although he was strapped in, or leaving Sarah stranded at the top. Someone kindly offered to help me. I watched her tip the buggy back and push it onto the moving stairs. From then on, it was a cinch. I would continue this trip once a fortnight when I went to see my Avon ladies.

It wasn't long before I found London had much more to offer than Crawley. The women were more than just caregivers for children. Their husbands were lawyers, stockbrokers, accountants, and police officers. Sarah went to a playschool five mornings a week, while Richard and I went to a toddler group in Finsbury Park run by a lady who became a good friend of mine. Her youngest daughter, Susie, became Richard's best friend.

Sylvia, whose husband, Tom, was our first babysitter when William fell down the manhole, introduced me to a few of her friends and neighbours. She was part of a large social circle in our area, which included the babysitting service, many toddler groups where mothers and young children could have fun and stay warm, and a wholesale food Co-op where we bought dried fruit, nuts, and legumes in bulk.

On Monday afternoons, the children and I joined other members of our new social group in the toy room at the Brownswood Library. The toys were good quality activity games, including Fisher-Price mobiles for infants, pull-along/push-along toys for just walking children, and trains, cars, and puzzles for all ages. We could sign out a toy and take it home for the week. Sarah was in seventh heaven. She loved dolls, but she always wanted a red, sit-on car. They had one.

The Regent Park Zoo was another great favourite for us. After the first time we went, I bought a family pass for the year. It cost only £6, which was a great value. Nowadays, a ticket costs upwards of £20 for a single adult. Often, we were a group of three or four adults with at least eight children in tow. Usually, we went on a Friday and had a wonderful day. We returned home at three or four in the afternoon, before the rush hour on the underground. I would put the children straight in the bath, make them some dinner, and have them in bed by 6:30 p.m.

Once we moved to London, birthday parties for the children became three-day events. I baked three cakes for each child, following a recipe book I had for fancy-decorated cakes. One cake went to school with the birthday child, one for a family celebration with grandparents, aunts, uncles and their children, and the last was for a local children's party. There were often many children around our dining table.

Sarah's fourth birthday was the first one celebrated at Prah Road—it was special. As the children arrived for the party, I discovered some uninvited guests in the wheel well of our car. The children and adults crowded around to prevent escapees as William collected a mother duck and six duckings before they got onto the road. With William in the lead, carrying a cardboard box full of feathers and down, he was accompanied by cheeps and quacks from the box and loud, excited chatter from the children. They followed him in their party clothes like the Pied Piper across Finsbury Park Road, into the park, and up the hill to the lake. I brought up the rear so as not to lose any stragglers. We all gathered at the lake's edge and watched as the fluffy ducklings followed their mother into the water. It was the perfect party entertainment. Then we went home to Prah Road for sandwiches and cake.

Before my third child was born in 1980, we made a few day trips to the coast, and one to France as a family of four. We also took a week-long trip to visit Thea and Sophie, who had moved to Newcastle. While there, we visited the Village of Beamish—the recently open-air living museum and a replica of a northern town during the early 20th century. Everyone had a wonderful day until we attempted to go down the Mahogany Drift Mine. Richard loved the hard hat but refused to go further than the gate into the mine—it was dark and wet. Sarah continued with her father to the coal face, where the height of the tunnel was only four feet.

In the spring of 1981, I took a week away from home to participate in my first group writing experience. I traveled to Lumb Bank, the home of poet Ted Hughes, who was married to Sylvia Plath. I don't recall where William and the children were during that time, but I had a wonderful experience. I wrote several poems and a story about preparing to leave my childhood home in St. Vincent.

Inspiration

We are all here for the week
In the remote Yorkshire Dales
Where memories will be
Entrusted to paper.
The Arvon Writing Foundation
The once home of Ted Hughes.
Fragments of hallucinatory dreams
Shroud my thoughts,
Time like the sunrise
On the yellow-dotted slope
Rolls up the crumpled
Layers of the night.

In the summer of 1981, we took another family holiday to a market town in the north of the county of Suffolk called Eye. We stayed in a renovated old farmhouse cottage. It was delightful. I don't remember much about that week, except that the stairs to the loft where we slept creaked with every twist and turn, and we had to carry the smaller children up and down those stairs, and that I took long walks along the village lanes.

Once, I passed my driving test, I was free to explore many other places. One of the unusual places my daughter remembers visiting is London's most famous cemetery, in Highgate. It is known for its beauty and notable residents. Although she was a young child at the time, she still recalls some of the fascinating stories we were told about the famous people buried there. One story was about Bram Stoker's inspiration for Dracula: wandering through the cemetery at dusk, he observed a family working in a glass-covered tomb. Numerous films have been shot around the architectural highlights of the Gothic cemetery, particularly the Egyptian Avenue, which leads into the Circle of Lebanon, a stunning structure of twenty sunken tombs built around the roots of an ancient Cedar of Lebanon tree, believed to predate the cemetery by over a hundred years.

Becoming Untethered

We had been working on Prah Road for almost two years. In September of 1980, Anne returned to England from traveling in Europe. She had been away for many months and asked if she could stay with us for a while before returning to Canada. Regrettably, Anne loved her cigarettes and gin and tonic—we barely drank, and the smoke was awful if she refused to go outside. I was afraid of confrontation and asked William to talk to her about it, but his reply, "She's your sister," meant he wouldn't ask, and I never found the courage to talk to Anne. I didn't want her mad at me.

This incident was one of many things that affected our lives. Neither William nor I knew how to handle our anger, sexual frustration, and exhaustion. Incidents compounded into each other. We were burgled twice. The first time, Sarah and Richard ran into the house ahead of me, wanting to watch television, while I brought David and the buggy into the hall. That's when I noticed the small window in the upper part of the kitchen was shattered. I panicked and raced up the stairs as the children ran back down, shouting, "Mummy, Mummy, the television isn't in the room."

I was terrified that the burglars were still in the house, but they must have jumped out of the first landing window when I put my keys in the door because only the television was taken. I was even more upset when I called William. I was trembling with fright, but he hung up on me. I called back. His answer to my questions was, "I hung up because you were getting hysterical."

He was probably correct, but the interaction left me feeling abandoned and emotionally hurt. I felt neither of us was happy. I started saving my small earnings for the future—but it never worked. The bank refused my request to open an account in my name— they required my husband's signature. Whenever William needed money for something important like the car, he asked me for money, and I gave him what I had—I couldn't refuse.

I remember praying William would find someone else and leave me; then I would have the house. I dreamt of getting away from our marriage and meeting someone interested in books and plays, someone who would take me to the theatre. I wasn't interested in a sexual relationship—I was always frustrated and in pain with William.

I felt differently about sex when I discovered some Playboy magazines in the back of the airing cupboard. At first, I was angry at William for hiding them in a place where the children might find them. Then, I wondered if sex was the reason behind our problems. I locked myself in the bathroom and read. I was surprised by my body's reactions to the stories. I became aroused like never before until I reached a climax and had an orgasm. I had never felt that kind of pleasure before, although we had been married for almost ten years. If only we could experience that euphoric feeling together, I felt sure our lives would be better.

Our sex life did change, but I never felt that climactic euphoria again, with one exception. Christmas 1981, we stayed in a cottage in Slapton, Devon, instead of at the Old Library—Mummy couldn't handle the noise of three young children. In bed, William displayed a desire for me that I hadn't experienced before. It was the marital bliss I wanted. I was aroused and had my first—and only—orgasm with William. I never stopped to question why, after ten years of marriage, William had never experimented sexually with me before or asked if I was OK.

Sadly, shortly after we came home, there was an incident over a parcel William was putting together for Sally, his brother Christopher's wife. I had forgotten to give William a list to put inside the box. Suddenly, he was yelling at me, calling me names. I was confused, bewildered, and had no idea what I had done wrong. Four years later, William would tell me he had been planning to leave us for another woman. William must have been under great emotional pressure with the thoughts of staying or leaving, which caused him to erupt when I forgot to give him the list! I closed down emotionally after that incident—the sudden change from love to anger was painful. My fears of being abandoned and my trust in William broke. I was ready to leave the relationship but hung on because I wasn't financially independent.

In July 1981, a month before our fantastic driving spree, the race riots from the Brixton uprising had spread to numerous other areas of London. We were following the news when we heard an uproar in our streets. The police, armed with riot shields and truncheons, had positioned themselves across the wide convergence of our three roads, ready to respond to violence with violence.

It was a terrifying experience. William's practical solution to close the front of the house and move to the back was reassuring but didn't quell my fears of a glass bottle or rock flying through our front window. We spent the time quietly reading or watching television with the children. The following day, only the mess was left—horse manure, broken bottles, and sticks. There was even a TV-sized hole in an upstairs window across the street, the broken parts lying on the pavement. Graham, William's friend from Hazlewick, was the only person who called to see if we were OK.

Decorating

Back in 1973, when William and I moved into our first home in Oulton Walk, Crawley, I had learnt to hang wallpaper. Neither of us had done this task before. We went shopping, found the paper we liked, and bought a pasting table, a large brush and pasting glue, scissors, a plumb-line, and a square brush to remove the air bubbles after the paper was on the wall. We were ready to work together.

The first piece was easy. We congratulated ourselves. William pasted and put the paper on the wall, and I used the big, clean brush to remove all the air bubbles. But, by the time we had lined up the pattern for the second piece, cut and pasted, and started lining it up, William walked away, saying, "I'm not going to do this, it's up to you if you want to paper the room." I don't remember an argument, just him leaving the room and shutting himself in his office. By the time he reappeared, I had successfully finished the one wall.

I found it a time-consuming and sticky job. It had been my first lesson learning that if I wanted something done, I'd have to do it myself. I also remember thinking that I never wanted to paper a wall again! Unfortunately, having walls plastered to a smooth finish in London was expensive, but using textured white paper was an alternative. This type of paper hid the cracks and bumps I was unable to smooth out completely. After tearing down the lathe and plaster walls and re-plastering, the papering and painting were a cinch in comparison.

In Prah Road, I did one room at a time. Once William had finished the behind-the-scenes work. I began cleaning and patching the walls with plaster. Then I wallpapered once the children were in bed. On Fridays and Saturdays, I worked until midnight, occasionally, even later, to try and finish a room. I worked on the children's bedrooms while Sarah was at school, and Richard and my child-minding charges napped in the playroom.

William left the choice of colour, design, and furnishings to me—He said that was my job. Since leaving Oulton Walk, he had taken on paying the bills as well as the mortgage, and I did the finishing and decorating of each room. I completed the plastering, wallpapering, painting, curtains, carpet, and door furnishings, all for about £100 a room; I was proud of myself. There were two exceptions—the curtains I hung in the living and dining room came from the Laura Ashley store in the West End of London. They were the most expensive curtains I have ever owned. I remember paying £300 for the curtains in the bay window of the living room. It was a lot of money, even back then, but over forty years later, I have those curtains still hanging and in good condition.

My final challenge was wallpapering the hall and the eighteen-foot stairwell. It was a daunting task. At the time, I was seven months pregnant and minding two other children. I was driven to have the house fully livable by the time I gave birth to our third child. I can scarcely recall how I balanced on the scaffolding boards, which William had secured for me, eighteen feet above the first floor, and painted the ceiling. Or how I managed to paste and hang the hall paper. I knew I had to find the money to pay a contractor or do it myself.

Not on the 6th!

It was Guy Fawkes Night—the 5th of November 1980. We went as a family to Alexandra Palace, Ally Pally as it was called, to watch the fireworks display. This pregnancy was different from the previous two. I had been content, busy finishing the house, sewing, and child-minding for extra money. I was already ten days past my due date, but wasn't worried because I was late in my previous pregnancies—eighteen days with the first and fourteen with the second.

I stood with my five-and-a-half-year-old daughter on a backless bench beside William, who carried three-year-old Richard on his shoulders. "Look, Mummy, look!" Sarah shouted with glee as the fireworks whooshed and showered starlights into the sky. Holding onto her, we leaned further and further back to follow the stars to the ground. Suddenly, I was falling with Sarah in my arms. My small stature and large protrusion out front caused me to overbalance. I hit the cold, damp ground with a thud.

"Mummy, are you OK?" Sarah asked, concern in her eyes.

"Yes, I'm fine, just a bit queasy." I could see my son's eyes widen in his round, cherubic face as William set him down on the ground and helped me up.

"Oh, that shook things up, I think," I groaned slightly, holding my back as I stood up straight.

"We'd probably should make a move for home, then," William said.

"No, no, let's finish watching the fireworks. I won't stand on the bench again," I laughed. We left soon after. The night was fog-drenched and smelling of gunpowder. It was about 8:00 p.m. It took an hour before we reached home and put the children to bed.

I had a dull pain for the rest of the evening and into the next day with some light contractions. But I kept saying to myself, "Not on the 6th." That was my father-in-law's birthday, and I wanted my baby to have its special day. I took a lovely hot bath in the evening and sat on one of the stools in the upper part of the kitchen in my dressing gown, drinking a cup of tea and mending my moccasin slippers, ready to go into the hospital. My doctor did not believe in home births.

William and Anne had gone to bed. I finished sewing, then thought I should call my midwife—she would decide when I needed to go to the hospital. In answer to her query, I told her my contractions were irregular, sometimes ten minutes apart, sometimes twenty, and I wasn't in any pain. "I'll get ready and come over," she said. I did not have regular contractions, In my previous births, they had always been all over the place.

I hung up the phone, which was situated on the corner wall of the kitchen, and walked down the two steps into the lower area to get a glass of water. I never reached the sink. My water broke, and the baby's head crowned immediately. With my legs apart, I staggered back up the steps and called out breathlessly, "Anne, Anne, come quickly. Hurry, pleeease!" I have always wondered why I didn't call for William. Anne had been drinking gin and tonics all evening and had also taken sleeping pills before going to bed. I think it was because, medically, I trusted her. She was a great nurse as well as a midwife.

Anne came rushing down the stairs, her hair askew and her dressing gown tied loosely around her middle, "Lord and mercy, what is the matter? You'll wake the household." I heard her take a deep breath as she came off the last step, "Oh, my dear God." I stood, knees bent, hanging on the wall. What she said next made me panic, "You have to lie down now."

I remember wailing, "I can't. I still have my knickers on!" I couldn't comprehend how to take them off.

"Just do it," Anne retorted sharply. "This baby's going to be born any minute. I'll be struck from the medical register. I haven't practised midwifery for twenty-plus years!"

It was my turn to be practical, "Don't be silly. This is an emergency, and you are my sister, aunt, whatever. You are family."

I was lying in the hallway, my head in the kitchen, my body between the front door and the bicycles, stroller, and large wicker cat basket, when I felt the baby sliding out of my body. The cats appeared curious about what was happening but never left their comfortable bed. I felt amused by my situation and a little concerned that this wasn't the cleanest place to have a baby.

"It's a boy!" Anne cried, asking for scissors and something to tie the umbilical cord.

"On the table," I said, waving at the counter behind me, where I had been sitting.

"Oh, my God, my watch is upstairs. What time was he born?"

"It's 1:00 a.m.," I replied, glancing up at the clock above the washing machine in the lower kitchen. I smiled to myself. It was the 7th of November, my baby had his own birthday.

It was the easiest of my three births—no stitches or drugs. Anne tied the umbilical cord with the string I used to repair my slippers and cut the cord with the kitchen scissors. There had not been time to grab towels or boil water. I remember thinking that his sliding from my body seemed to go on forever. I saw Anne tip the baby upside down. Then he cried. Relief washed over me. Anne wrapped the baby in the bath towel I'd used to dry my hair, which lay on the counter with my moccasins and the empty tea cup.

I was sitting up, leaning against the cat basket, listening to their purring, when the assistant midwife knocked at the door. She was young and looked extremely flustered when she walked in, found me on the floor and Anne holding the baby. "Oh! I didn't expect the baby to be born. Weren't you supposed to give birth in the hospital?"

The midwife arrived immediately afterwards and took charge. I saw William appear in the now-lit hallway looking confused and sleepy—the doorbell had woken him. The midwife decided I didn't have to go to the hospital because no stitches were needed. I don't remember the afterbirth coming away or the mess on the floor being cleaned. All I cared about was that I had

249

a healthy baby boy. David was twenty-four inches long and eight pounds and four ounces in weight.

I heard the midwife tell William to bring a bed downstairs and set it up in the living room with the crib alongside for the baby. I'm sure I was removed from the dusty hall floor and placed in a chair in the living room and blankets placed around me, but I remember nothing more until the bed was made up, and William helped me get in.

Anne must have made tea and prepared a bottle—the baby steriliser was by the sink. I was handed the bottle and David. Someone had already bathed and dressed him. I remember being thankful that we had recently laid the carpet and hung the curtains in what had once been our garage room. I was also relieved that Anne was there for me. I knew she would look after me. I don't remember sleeping much or William saying anything other than to thank Anne for being there and delivering the baby.

Around seven in the morning, we heard Richard screaming. William had brought his bed downstairs in the middle of the night, having first placed Richard in our bed. I can't imagine what went through his mind when he awoke; we weren't there, and his bed was gone—poor little boy. William ran upstairs to pick him up and bring him down. Richard's lip quivered as he crawled into my lay with his thumb in his mouth. It was a few days before he asked any questions about the baby. The main ones being, "How did he get out?" And, "Did he get stuck in your knickers?" Which made me laugh as I tried to explain details he would understand.

Later, I added to Richard's traumatic experience—I thought it was for the best—by sending Richard to play school. For the first time in three years, he was difficult to handle. It was a big mistake. He was the dearest little boy and must have felt sadly neglected. Sarah, once awake, was transfixed by the tiny infant asleep in the crib. She was excited and eager to go to school and tell her friends about her baby brother.

Life in Prah Road was difficult after David was born. William had taken a week off to help at home after I had my first child and three days with the second, but he took no time off from work to help out after David's birth. I think he reasoned that Anne was still with us. But I wanted the care, comfort, and understanding from William as well.

Although I enjoyed most of Anne's visit, she was never easy to be around because of her drinking and smoking. The only time William and I spent time together alone, we were exhausted by our frustration with Anne. We were very grateful for her delivering David but were also happy when she left a few weeks after he was born. She returned to Canada to be near her daughter Jeanne-Marie, who lived in a group home in Trenton, Ontario.

Breaking Points

Looking back, I believe William knew our marriage was failing, but like me, he didn't know what to do about it. Neither of us had any background in resolving problems or family or friends to turn to who might help. Both of us had witnessed the belittling of a spouse, and William had seen physical violence between his parents. I grew up, as a child, hearing, "You've made your bed, now lie in it," which meant I had to accept the consequences of my action: we were married, and marriage was supposed to be forever. It would take another four years of incidents and trying to move forwards before the final break in our marriage.

We did not go down to Devon for Christmas of 1980. David was just over a month old and sick. It was Christmas Eve when I finally called the doctor because I was extremely worried. I was amazed by his quick arrival, still dressed in formal evening attire. "Your son is seriously ill, he has acute pneumonia."

I was angry at myself for listening to William, who'd dismissed my worries saying, "You are just being neurotic." But I was furious with William. I swore I'd never listen to him about the children again. Our baby nearly died.

Not long afterwards, William decided to participate in the Royal Marine Regiment TA (Territorial Army), now called the Royal Marine Reservists. He was required to shave his facial hair. Probably as a joke, he went to a barber instead of shaving at home—it backfired. He surprised me by coming through the front door and attempting to kiss me. All I saw was a stranger in my house, and screamed. I did eventually laugh, but the scare left me shaken. I would have at least been prepared for the change if William had discussed his decision with me, but he didn't, and if he'd cuddled me instead of laughing at my fear, I would have responded more kindly. A few weeks later, William received a couple of cracked ribs when caught between two burly men. He quit the TA shortly afterwards. His pride was damaged as much as the bruises and broken bones.

Still hurt by his lack of communication, I wasn't sympathetic and heard Mummy's caustic sarcasm come out of my mouth when he came home injured. "It's your fault." I'd never understood his choice to join in the first place. I knew it wasn't patriotism. I was angry and fearful of his choice. For William, I had fallen short of his ideal woman. In a letter written to me in 1970 while I was still in the Caribbean, he wrote:

> *My ideal female would not be as tall as me,*
> *have short curly hair, blue eyes, and lovely lips.*
> *She would be able to darn, sew, and cook and*
> *an understanding that bears a great deal of*
> *sympathy should I need it.*

When the Falklands War started in April 1982, his choice returned to haunt me. If he were called up to fight, I'd be left with three small children and no means to support us. I was terrified. In my fear and anger, I berated William for signing up for something that could get him killed. I didn't understand why he couldn't have chosen a sport less military. I had many nightmares during those ten weeks of disturbance.

About this time, William told me he was starting a program of hypnosis but didn't say why or what the purpose was. He insisted he had to be alone, in bed, to listen to the tapes, which meant I often couldn't go to bed until after midnight. I wonder now if the story about hypnosis was a cover for sexual tapes because one afternoon, I disturbed him during a nap, and he flew into a rage. He said I'd woken him from the perfect sexual dream!

Sarah's teacher called for a conference to discuss the family situation. "Does Sarah have a father?" She asked. "Sarah only writes about you, her brothers, Auntie Anne, but never about her father." I was shocked. After supper that night, once the children were in bed, I told William about the conference and begged him to become more involved in the children's care.

All our anger and pent-up frustrations came to a head one late morning. William was on his way to bed after working Friday night as a security guard, and I was frustrated and lonely. Without thinking, I started vacuuming, and William shouted at me. "Could you not make such a racket."

"Couldn't you help me? We'll get it done faster, and then we can relax together." I replied sharply.

William stomped upstairs, slamming the bedroom door. Trembling with nervous energy, I ran up after him, angry at being cut off. As I entered our room, William pushed me and shouted, "Leave me alone!"

The next thing I remember was waking up in bed, the three children standing at the headboard crying. William was upset and in tears, possibly terrified of what, in his anger, he'd done. I was astonished when he took my Bible and swore he'd never raise his hand to me again—He was an acclaimed atheist. Still, I believed him. William said, I tumbled down the stairs and hit my head on the wall, but I found broken pieces of his beer glass inches away from where my head had made a dent in the wall. Had he thrown it before or after I fell? I wondered.

William was always solicitous after an incident. This time, he suggested we start looking at buying a small house that didn't need major renovations. He said, "The housing market is good, and we are in a great position to purchase a smaller house. We can buy without a mortgage after selling Prah Road, decorate the interior, and in three years, sell and move out to the country."

I was happy. If we relocated to the suburbs before David started school, it would be better for our children, and our marriage might survive. We thought we'd found the right house in Haringey. A two-storey, three-bedroom home that needed only interior painting. It had a small garden and easy public transportation for William to work and the children to school. We put our house on the market, and the first person through the door made us a good offer.

I reminded William of the trouble we'd had with London estate agents. I urged him to go directly to the seller of the house in Haringey, who we knew was interested in a quick sale, to see whether our offer was acceptable. Unfortunately, William delayed and when we went to the house, we saw the owner's son, who informed us that his father had died, and the price had now increased. William was angry, and I had to pull him away from the front door.

I was exasperated at William. He'd refused to listen to my suggestion, and now we'd lost the deal. I had such high hopes for a happy solution, and the loss of the house contributed to a growing depression. Nothing gave me joy; I just performed my daily duties of cooking, cleaning, and caring for the children.

During another argument, I ran up the stairs after William but recalled the previous incident and crumpled at his feet. "I give up. You win," I said. Fear radiated through my body as I fell to my knees. In the split-second I entered the room, I realised that if the bedroom window had been open, I might have jumped through it. What would have happened if I had jumped?

I got up slowly and walked downstairs— William did not attempt to stop me. I opened the bathroom cabinet and purposefully took a handful of antihistamines and another of Paracetamol (Tylenol). They were the only pills we had. All I wanted was oblivion at that moment. I do not remember William asking or me telling him what I had taken. But he must have guessed because he insisted I stay awake. He put us all in the car, drove us to a park, and kept me walking until I was no longer drowsy.

I kept going, but emotionally, I was lost. Why was William always so kind after an incident and never before?

Moving Again

We still had a buyer for Prah Road, and they were willing to wait until we found another house. It wasn't long before we saw a lovely Edwardian house on a quiet street. It was near a railway line. It was still in Hackney, but William's mother thought it was a better move, more upscale than Prah Road or Haringey. With this house, we would have a mortgage rather than paying for it outright and not have the extra money if we had moved to the little house in Haringey.

It took nine months of worry and stress before we signed the papers and moved into Parkholme Road. The chain of buyers and sellers was long, and one was tied up in Probate. I felt compelled to step in again over the heads of the solicitors and estate agents and deal directly with the buyers and sellers. One said, "We'll sign when we return from holiday."

I took a deep breath and before I could stop myself, replied, "No, you won't. We have been waiting nine months for you. Please sign immediately, or we will drop out, and there will be many unhappy people." Two days later, the papers were signed, and we began packing. We had two weeks before leaving on a family holiday.

It was the summer of 1982. My in-laws had arranged a camping trip to Guernsey in the Channel Islands for the four of us, plus William's sister, Susan, her husband, and their two children, who were similar in age to ours. It was a lovely holiday, especially for the children. I believed June and Bill hoped taking us on a holiday would ease our stress.

On our return to England, we drove directly to Devon, where we dropped Sarah off to spend time with Lorna and her grandmother. She would stay for a week while we moved house. Back in London, I took Richard the next morning to a school friend for the weekend. David went to another friend with a child the same age but unfortunately couldn't stay overnight. This would cause enormous stress on the family for the best part of the following year.

William and I worked hard that day. Once again, we were expecting help, this time from William's co-workers. But no one turned up. We moved everything out of the house at Prah Road into a three-tonne truck and our car. We were on the road to our new home by 8:00 p.m. We stopped to collect David on the way. I was still running on adrenaline, but could see that William was white with fatigue. "Why don't you take David upstairs, fix the sleeping bags, and go to bed? I'll empty the car, and then we can have tea in the morning before starting on the truck."

"I am exhausted, thanks."

I crawled into my sleeping bag on the floor with David wedged between us when I was finished. Awake by 6:00 a.m., I helped David dress, we had a quick breakfast, and I left him playing with a few toys I had brought. We unloaded our remaining belongings by 10:00 a.m., except for a large freezer, which sat outside the front door for three days—I'd refused to take it any further. While David stayed with William, I drove the truck back to the old house. I smiled as I navigated a tiny winding alley, thrilled with my driving skills. I picked up our rabbit, Benji. He had spent the night outside the front door of Prah Road in his cage. I took a quick look around the house, smiling with pleasure at the work we had done to restore the place but also with deep sadness. Our lives had changed so much since we moved from Crawley, and not always for the best. Although I didn't hold out much hope, I prayed for things to improve and returned to our new home.

While William returned the truck, David and I wandered into the garden at Parkholme Road. We agreed on a place to put Beni's cage when William returned. I unpacked the kitchen boxes and made lunch for the three of us. We were busy until late afternoon, with David following us closely until I laid him down for an early nap.

When I took David to collect Richard, I was disconcerted by his reaction when he saw his brother. He flung his arms around Richard, sobbing. Much later, I wondered if he thought we had lost Richard with the move. We picked Sarah up from the train station a couple of days later. It wasn't such a dramatic greeting—I must have talked more about Sarah coming home than Richard. But I could tell that David was relieved we were all together again.

1982–1988
Parkholme Road

Parkholme Road

With the move, I gave up childminding—my charges and my youngest would be in playschools. But to help our finances—now that I could drive—I took a job as a nursing assistant in the Camden district, working from 7:00 to 11:00 p.m. The job entailed taking care of the infirm and elderly who needed assistance in their homes at night. When I worked, William put the children to bed. I also applied and was accepted as a host mother for American Heritage overseas students—the first two would arrive in the spring of 1983. They came to England to study for three months at a time, and it paid well.

Our new house was clean and well-built. It required only a little modernizing. William's first task was adding more plug sockets in the top bedroom, where the students would sleep. We had an interesting first meeting with our neighbours while working in that room. William was busy cutting into the walls, and neither of us had checked the time. During a pause, we heard yelling. We opened the window to see a whiskered face screaming for us to be quiet. It was close to midnight, and William's sawing on the adjoining wall shook the houses. We were most apologetic.

We were happy to discover that another of our neighbours was a contractor, and his brother worked for the gas company. William hired them to make other changes we wanted done. I began painting once William finished the wiring and the floor was nailed down securely. I would not be wallpapering in this house.

I worked on the house during the day while David was at playschool and later napped. When Sarah and Richard came home from school, we had tea and cake and watched television for an hour before homework, baths, and dinner.

Sarah had attended Dallington, a private school, for two years. Anne had insisted, saying, "Lorna and I will pay two-thirds of the cost." Our expense at the time was only £60. Sarah thrived at Dallington, and although we would now pay an additional £200, William and I thought it beneficial for Richard to attend as well.

During the first week in our new home, David began behaving irrationally, and I noticed he had four raised and scabbed bumps on his back along his waistline. I took him to the doctor's surgery at the end of our road, but at the first sight of the doctor, David went crazy, screaming and struggling. Surprised and worried, I visited my former doctor in Finsbury Park. I should have known better, but at least the doctor diagnosed his condition. "It is shingles. It will go away," he reassured me. "However, you are no longer in my jurisdiction. You will need to find a doctor in your neighborhood. Goodbye, and best of luck."

Although the blisters disappeared the following week, I still had to figure out how to handle David's erratic behaviour. He screamed and cried most of the time when he wasn't asleep. He wouldn't sit still and eat at the dinner table unless I fed him. He constantly dropped his knife and fork as though his fingers didn't work correctly. He also took to falling on the floor, saying, "I'm stuck." At first, I made a game of it. He'd raise an arm, and I'd pull. If it didn't work, I'd pretend to shovel him up. He might laugh a little, give me a coy smile, and be happy for a while, but the situation didn't improve.

William became irritated by what he thought were silly games and constant interruptions at the table. "Stop the mollycoddling. Leave him at the table to finish or send him to bed without supper a few times."

"He's got to eat," I said.

I hated the idea of this particular discipline, even though Thea and Mummy said the same thing. This wasn't a case of him not liking the food but something different. It was difficult to balance William's irritation, my need to get jobs done, and David's behaviour. Ordinary tasks took much longer to complete. I was exhausted, angry, and worried.

I learnt more about shingles by talking with a fellow nurse. She explained that although the virus is not common in children, extreme stress on the emotional and nervous systems can activate the virus, and those who had chickenpox before the age of one year were more at risk—David had chickenpox with the rest of the children when he was only six months old. Then, there was the obvious stress when he was separated from his brother during the move. There was no medical solution, only patience, which was limited for all of us. But the knowledge was a great help and made it easier for me to cope.

The Next Three Years

O ver the next three years, William and I worked on improving the home; he hired Brian, the neighbour, to remodel the kitchen and pantry. It was my job to deal with the finishing work—I used strong chemicals to remove the paint from the beautiful pitch pine doors and mahogany staircase and an electrical steamer to remove the layers of wallpaper before painting. Underneath the paint, in one room, was an exquisite, thin veneer of rolled walnut wood. In the large room that became our kitchen, the Edwardian crown molding was beautiful under all the years of paint. Working above my head from the top of a ladder, I managed to strip eighteen inches at a time to reveal the intricate floral design underneath.

Our first two students were Peter and Andy; Peter came from New York, and Andy from Bellingham. They were as different as "chalk and cheese," as Mummy would say. I became close with Andy, a gentle, kind, twenty-four-year-old theatre student. He changed the trajectory of my life. He introduced me to incredible theatre, motivated the children to be bold and adventurous, and encouraged me to enter the academic world. Joy returned to my life. His offers of help astounded me—he watched the children in the bath, helped prepare meals, and, best of all, noticed things I liked—drinking my coffee before leaving the table after dinner. William never did—he went so far as to say, "I know what you want, but I'm not doing it," when I asked him why, which left me feeling emotionally abandoned.

The day after an incident in the kitchen when William gave Andy a concert ticket, saying in front of me, "You might like this. Jane won't want to go." I was amazed and thrilled when Andy approached me. "I could see how much you wanted to be asked. I exchanged the ticket William gave me for two matinee tickets. Will you go with me? We'll get back before the kids come home from school."

It was the most beautiful music I'd ever heard—Handel's *Messiah*. By the time the concert was finished, our tears had mingled on the backs of our hands. My heart was beating with joy. Going to concerts and the theatre was the beginning of a love affair with classical music, and Andy.

During Andy's stay with us, I saw an advertisement in a local paper for an Access Course: a year's study allowing a person access to a London college. I had dreamt of getting a degree. But William wasn't encouraging, saying, "You won't have time; you have three children and a house to look after."

When I showed it to Andy, his eyes lit up with excitement. "My mother is going back to school. You'll find it thrilling," he said.

I applied using my first name, Elizabeth, instead of Jane and didn't tell William about it until I was accepted. I was ecstatic. Even though Andy left our home before I started the Access Course and William wasn't thrilled about me attending college, I refused to be deterred.

The Access Course was incredible. Fifteen students started, and eight entered North London Polytechnic in

Camden a year later. I was one of five who finished the BA course. I spent most of the night struggling to write my first essay, but my tutor, whom I called in the middle of the night, sobbing, was right when she said, "You can do it." I was exuberant with my achievement when I went to school the following morning after only one hour of sleep. My independence and sense of identity grew during this period.

After a relatively mild argument, William took off for a couple of weeks, leaving me with the kids. I enjoyed the space but was sad that the children didn't notice or ask where Daddy was. When William called and asked to meet at a pub alongside the canal, I agreed. William greeted me with a smile and said, "I ordered you a cider," when I arrived.

"Thanks," I replied with a half smile. If he'd given me a choice, I would have chosen a shandy (lemonade and lager). I found myself adding up the times he didn't give me an option.

We talked a little about the house and the children but not about the real crux of our problems—the feelings of emotional abandonment and hurt on both sides. We did not understand each other's needs. He suggested we get a puppy. I was hesitant, thinking of the work involved in having a dog. Trying to be kind, I said, "The children will like that."

The next Saturday morning, William drove the children and me to the pet shop. He went in and came out with a puppy. I enjoyed the children's excited faces, but all I thought was, now I had more to care for.

End of Our Marriage

Our last altercation occurred just before my thirty-fifth birthday in 1985. I was upstairs writing a paper for my class. I had taken over the up-stairs bedroom as my study—it gave me space, which I thought William would understand—he had done the Open University (OU) course for the first six years of our marriage. But secretly, it made me feel closer to Andy, whose presence in my life still felt like a gift from God. My early achievements in the Access Course had made me bolder and more assertive.

The children were in bed, and William was downstairs with Jobi, the new puppy. We didn't let him go upstairs. Suddenly, William burst into the room. Jobi had made a mess on the hall floor, and William had accidentally stepped in it. After all the years I had shouted back, this time I didn't. I looked at William and said calmly, "You told me you would take care of the dog tonight while I studied." His rage left the room in disarray—books and papers scattered everywhere and a hole in the wall where he'd thrown my sewing machine.

I spent the night reflecting on my marriage: This altercation wasn't caused by an argument. Each interaction I had experienced with William was worse than the last. This time, he'd had his hands around my throat as he dragged me from my chair. If I stayed married, what would happen next?

I realised I couldn't be compliant again. I wouldn't argue, nor would I run away. I had to take control of my life and move on. The next morning, I came downstairs to find flowers in a vase and a note asking for my forgiveness, "To turn back the clocks to our little house in Crawley." As much as I cared for William as a person I'd loved and the father of our children, I was afraid and no longer respected him—he had sworn on the Bible never to hit me again—I felt we were completely broken.

I did two things that morning once the children left for school. I went to my doctor to have the bruises on my neck documented and to my adviser at the London Polytechnic. She gave me a list of marriage guidance counsellors, and I went to see one. I was allowed six free sessions. After the first two, I asked William if he would be willing to come with me, but he refused. One night, I had a dream. I stood on the ground, dressed in white, my arms at my sides. Then, I was transformed into a beautiful bird, soaring higher and higher into the sky. My wings opened, and I flew away. It was powerful. I read that the dream represented freedom and peace. I knew what I had to do.

I still cooked and did laundry for William, but I slept separately. When we could finally sit calmly and talk, we discussed the situation. After tears and a few tentative embraces, I eventually said, "It will not work, us living in the same house together, the tension is too great. But you can stay until you find a place."

Two months later, we had one last Christmas together with the children. It was friendly and pleasant, with only a little tension. The children stayed up late. I remember David climbing into my lap and falling asleep mid-sentence at 1:00 a.m.

After breakfast, William suggested that he and I walk along the river without the children. He talked amicably about his plans for the future. He agreed to move out at the beginning of the New Year. He wanted to live on a houseboat, paint in his spare time, and have visitation rights with the children every other weekend. I would be responsible for the children, pets, and the house until it was sold. He voluntarily offered to pay £150 for maintenance. My feelings were: if William wanted his freedom, he could have it—I would manage. I would not disagree or demand anything—I didn't want an argument.

By the end of January 1986, I was worried because I'd applied for legal aid and received an income support check, which I couldn't cash because William was still living in the house. I was afraid to broach the subject with William, but my college adviser said, "You must go home and tell your husband he has to move out until the situation is resolved."

William said he would pack his personal belongings and leave in the morning. The contents of the home would be divided in the future. I didn't know where he lived for a while, but I remember being asked to sign legal papers for him to get a second mortgage on a houseboat. It was almost thirteen years since that exceptional day in February during a miner strike when the electrical power was restored as I reached the church doors. The magic had not held up against reality.

I was doing well at school and working hard to finish the house. My solicitor wanted to take the divorce proceedings to court and request more than £150 for three children. But I believed William when he said he would leave the country, and I'd get nothing. William eventually agreed to a seventy-thirty split in my favour, in the division of the property of Parkholme Road so we could live in a house, not a flat (apartment).

In the final decree, I was surprised when the judge awarded me sole custody of the children. He said, "As Mr. Wakeling has not appeared in court, he must not want his children." I never knew why William didn't show up. I hadn't asked for custody, but I was glad. As the only parent legally responsible for the children, my future decisions, like where they went to school or where we lived, would be easier.

Epilogue

William and I had known each other for over six years before our marriage. I saw him as my refuge, my knight in shining armour. I was bewitched by love, but in my naivety, I ignored some important differences. Our humour was very different. But more importantly, I should have questioned William's statement in a letter about his friend's trouble with his girlfriend: "*I told him to just bash her around a bit, and everything would be good.*"

After six years of doing everything together, I was stunned when he no longer held my hand. "There's no need—we're married now," he had said.

I have often wished I'd had the courage to tell him how I'd felt. Maybe our lives might have been different. Over our thirteen years of marriage, I felt slowly erased, hurt by William's lack of understanding and affection. Each time, I thought, it's not important, I don't need to sing in the bath if he's around. I should be able to let go of childhood books—I was a grown-up.

The move to London impacted me profoundly—I was proud of what I accomplished: renovating the house, managing the finances, and being responsible for the children. I wanted to be involved; it was also my home. What I didn't understand was William also had a fragile ego.

Andy's attitude changed me. He saw joy and love in everything. It reminded me of the love I felt as a child, sitting in an avocado tree in our backyard, watching the dragonflies hovering over the rain-filled cesspit, building paper sailing boats, and sending them down the flooded street with Daddy.

Although there were good moments in our marriage, in the end, it seemed that everything I had believed about William was a lie. I thought he loved me despite my faults. But he laughed off my loneliness and insecurities. My heart broke when on the morning he moved out of the house in Parkholme Road in 1986, he told me he had never wanted children.

About the time of my separation from William and our ultimate divorce, I visited the Tate Modern Art Gallery in London. The gallery houses a collection of international modern and contemporary art from the 1900s onwards. Most sculptures were large and housed singularly in a room. But the only piece I remember was in the entrance. The Tree* by Giuseppe Penone was

*https://giuseppepenone.com/en/words/trees

271

a twelve-metre (almost forty-foot), sculpture of a tree emerging from a large square block of wood, the ground support for the piece of art.

I have never forgotten that sculpture, recognising the concept of finding the tree within the wood. I began to understand that beneath all the ups and downs of my relationships—my birth mother and siblings, my husband and children, and my bereavements—there was still a core of me that was strong.

As a child, Daddy's method of endearment was to say, "You get uglier every day." I accepted the comment without understanding he meant the opposite. My grandmother, Mummy, thought cuddling was foolish. My birth mother called me a "cold fish" because I pulled away from being squeezed against her breast.

Before we were married, William wrote: "*You are lovable but hopeless—somewhat dogmatic, but I like the fascinating twinkle in your eyes.*" He also wrote that when I set my mind on an objective, "*You blunder through everything to get there.*"

My *dogmatic* nature and ability to persevere through anything propelled me to keep going. It saved me in my early days in England. It got me through college, my divorce, and the death of Mummy and Daddy. It also saved me when Andy left England to return home to Bellingham, Washington.

In the four years following my divorce, I rediscovered my strengths; I realised, I was creative in my own way—intelligent, determined, and accomplished. It made me relentless in whatever I wanted to do. I knew I had to push down the bad, hurt feelings and get on with my life. I had more social events during those four years than throughout the previous thirteen years of my marriage. I even went to Greece and Rome on my own.

Many exchange students stayed with us at Parkholme Road after William left. They came from all walks of life and places in America. Some were lovely, and we remained friends long after they had left England. Some were scary, like the girl from the Bronx, who, when I woke her up for a phone call—their families never could get the time difference right—shot up in her bed, putting her hands around my throat. I enjoyed hearing about their different lives and was envious of the girls receiving letters addressed with their first and last names. All my letters were addressed to Mrs W. F. Wakeling. I wanted desperately to have a letter addressed with my first name. It was always a thrill to receive Andy's letters, which came addressed with my given name.

At the beginning of my second year at college, 1986, following Mummy's death, I persuaded my professors that I could complete my BA if they let me work at my own pace. Despite my many stresses, I finished my BA degree and was awarded a second class honours (2:1)** in July 1989.

I also completed the renovations of Parkholme Road. Once it was sold, I bought and renovated another house on the Hackney Marshes and was accepted by Cambridge University, where I completed a diploma in education.

** Britisg degree classification: Second class honours, upper division(2.1): usually the average overall exam score of 60%+.

Juggling college and home was hard, especially for the children. I left home on a Monday morning after they had gone to school and returned on Friday afternoon just before them. During the weekend, I did the laundry, cleaned, cooked the meals for the rest of the week, and tried to complete my classwork. I did have a young male au pair, a friend from Bellingham, who wanted to come to England. Although, my thirteen-year-old daughter took more care of him than he did of them.

I did a three-month teachers' training placement at Plashet High School. It was an unforgettable experience teaching young Asian girls, some of whom were destined for arranged marriages at the age of fifteen.

In 1986, the summer before Mummy died, the children and I spent a month travelling across America from New York to Bellingham, Washington, where Andy still lived. Originally, he had planned to meet us in New York with a van I bought, and he lived in for a while. Although that plan fell through, I was determined enough to go ahead with my plans without him. I held on to the optimism and positive thread I had experienced with him.

I remember exiting the I-5 at Samish Road at the end of that trip and feeling I had finally come home. Although Andy and I were never together again, we did meet more than once in the future. We continued to write letters long after I had purchased a house and moved to Bellingham in October 1991 with my three children to begin a new adventure.

When I look back now, thirty-plus years later, I'm not sure what I was thinking, but I knew if I remained in England, I would drown. I had no reason to stay. Mummy and Daddy had passed. William and I were still unable to talk civilly to each other. My birth mother and I didn't communicate, and the British economy was going to hell in a handbasket. I wanted a better education for my children who were struggling under the British system. And a society that would allow me to grow.

High school sweethearts: Jane
Moller and William Wakeling.

Jane celebrating her 21st birthday with
William. October, 1970.

Jane in Cornwall shortly before her marriage. 1971.

William and Jane.

William and Jane's
engagement party,
October, 1970.

William and Jane,
Wedding Day. February 12, 1972.

Jane is chosen as Queen for the Day in a pageant celebrating the Queen's Silver Jubilee , 1977.

Jane's daughter, Sarah, at two and a half was Tinkerbell in the Jubilee parade. She won a Koala bear for best costume!

Richard at 2 and a half.

David and Jane,
1981.

Lynda with Sarah and Richard at her home,
September, 1978.

Sarah, Richard,
and David
at Prah Road, 1981.

Ice cream stop! Road trip after learning to drive.

College Days. Jane at a Greek party at
Parkholme Road.

Jane's 40th birthday party, 1989.
With her children she left for Bellingham,
Washington, soon after.

Postscript

This memoir, Untethered, *is about my traumas, fears, and aloneness amid family. Also, my successes and independence as I fought for them. My children, their father, and my mother will each have different views of my behaviour and actions. I do not judge them, as I hope they will not judge me, and ask their forgiveness for anything I have written that may offend them.*

Bonus Pages

Here's a Sneak Preview from

Chosen, A Memoir

BARBADOS

Early Years

According to my birth mother whom I didn't know until I was a young and immature teenager—I was conceived out of wedlock from a date rape in Barbados and born in a back room of a house in Bridport, England.

My grandmother came to England from the Caribbean on the pretence of being lonely and wanting to visit her daughters. She planned to adopt me without telling her husband I was his youngest daughter's child. My grandmother wanted to protect my mother and me from scandal. When my grandmother left England and took me back to Barbados, I was eleven months of age. I wouldn't hear from my mother again until I was over fourteen years old.

My grandmother and I flew BOAC (British Overseas Airways Corporation, a predecessor of British Airways) from London to Barbados with a stopover in Nassau, Bahamas. I was now my grandmother's daughter and would grow up calling her and my grandfather, Mummy and Daddy.

I slept most of the way to Nassau, even swallowing in my sleep to relieve ear pressure caused by the rapid air changes as the plane took off and landed.

"You've a natural flyer there, ma'am," the air hostess told Mummy, who loved to retell stories about bringing me home.

From all the letters written to her daughters, and sisters to sisters, and stories told by Mummy, I was a very happy child; I took everything in my stride and was as fit as a fiddle, one letter reported.

***

The Last Hurricane

Daddy got up in the morning to check on the damage outside. Our stony road was now a rushing six-foot-wide river! We worked together to return the house to normal, then I went to play in the river. The water, the colour of milky tea, rushed around my legs, almost pushing me over. I made paper boats with Daddy's help, sailing them off into the swirling waves, and had fun imagining them landing on foreign shores. Mummy baked, and we had fresh warm bread and butter with whatever was in the larder for breakfast, lunch, and dinner. I played for a few days in that milky-tea river, making elaborate boats of all styles and sizes until the water finally receded.

I still hold a tableau vision of Mummy: she is wearing a blue gingham dress, a white belt around her waist, and white sandals on her bare feet. She is standing on the top step of the front porch. She looks happy, smiling, and waving to Daddy and me, standing in the middle of the rushing water. I'm in a baby blue seersucker swimsuit, and Daddy is wearing khaki shorts, a pale yellow, frayed, short-sleeved shirt, and green gumboots.

For those few days, while the road was impassable, Mummy went about her daily life: making bread, reading, crocheting, and writing letters. Daddy, unable to go down to the store for a drink, stayed home and built boats for me.

What was called "A terrible act of God" seemed like an incredible gift to me.